M000087561

Gina Bates

EAT SLOW.
FAST COOKER RECIPES.

Healthy Eating

for a Good and Healthful Lifestyle

with Good Recipes in 30 minutes

A house
is not a home
unless it contains food and fire
for the mind as well as the body.
(Benjamin Franklin)

Table of Contents

Introduction   *1*

Chapter 1: Healthy Breakfast Recipes   *3*

Egg and Fried Rice Olé (Time: 15 minutes)   5

Breakfast Tacos (Time: 25 minutes)   11

Oven Denver Omelette (Time: 30 minutes)   17

Poached Egg and Beans (Time: 15 minutes)   20

Tofu Stir Fry (Time: 25 minutes)   25

Avocado Toast with Egg (Time: 10 minutes)   31

Southwestern Waffles (Time:13 minutes)   34

Savory Oatmeal with Cheddar and Fried Eggs
(Time: 10 minutes)   37

Zucchini Bread Oatmeal (Time: 13 minutes)   40

Skinny Spiced Coconut Yogurt Quinoa Muffins
(Time: 30 minutes)   43

Egg In a Nest (Time: 10 minutes)   47

Fast Hammy Grits (Time: 15 minutes)   50

Breakfast Nachos (Time: 25 minutes)   54

Hootsla (egg bread) (Time: 10 minutes)   57

Banana and Fromage Blanc Grilled Cheese
(Time: 15 minutes)   60

Chapter 2: Healthy Appetizer Recipes   63

Pastrami Roll-ups (Time: 15 minutes)   65

Poached Shrimp (Time: 30 minutes)   68

Tuna Lettuce Wraps (Time: 10 minutes)   72

Fig Toasties (Time: 10 minutes)   76

Chickpea and Red Pepper Dip (Time: 5 minutes) 80

Wild Salmon and Avocado Triangles
(Time: 8 to 10 minutes)   83

Peanut Hummus with Fruit and Veggie Sticks
(Time: 10 minutes)   86

Buckeye Balls (Time: 30 minutes)   89

Tuna Melt Sandwich (Time: 25 minutes)   93

Basil Chicken Banh Mi Sandwich
(Time: 30 minutes)   97

Salted Butterscotch and Pecan Cookies
(Time: 25 minutes)   102

German Vegetarian Tomato Spread
(Time: 30 minutes)   106

Five Layer Mexican Dip (Time: 23 minutes)   110

Polenta Squares with Mushroom Ragu
(Time: 30 minutes)   114

Chapter 3: Healthy Pasta Recipes   *118*

Chicken and Broccoli Alfredo
(Time: 20 minutes)   120

Garlic Lemon Shrimp with Pasta
(Time: 30 minutes)   124

Vegan Creamy Mushroom Pasta
(Time: 25 minutes)   127

Tuna Carbonara (Time: 30 minutes)   131

Penne all'Arrabbiata (Time: 20 minutes)   135

Ravioli with Sun-dried Tomatoes, Arugula and
Hazelnuts (Time: 15 minutes)   138

Hummus Linguini with Zucchini
(Time: 25 minutes)   141

Sweet Potato Noodles (Time: 25 minutes)   144

Chinese Noodles with Bok Choy and Hoisin Sauce
(Time: 30 minutes)   147

Marmite Carbonara (Time: 20 minutes)   151

Macadamia Pesto Pappardelle
(Time: 30 minutes)   154

Macaroni and Cheese Topped with Salsa
(Time: 25 minutes)   157

Lemon Pepper Pasta with Shrimp
(Time: 15 minutes)   160

Mushroom Spaghetti Aglio Olio
(Time: 15 minutes)   163

Creamy Salmon Orzo (Time: 15 minutes)   166

Lemon Butter Garlic Shrimp with Pasta
(Time: 15 minutes)   169

Penne Rosa (Time: 30 minutes)   172

Chapter 4: Healthy Salad Recipes   *175*

Romaine Salad with Lemon-Pecorino Vinaigrette
(Time: 20 minutes)   177

Healthy Coleslaw (Time: 10 minutes)   179

Black Bean Mango Salad (Time: 15 minutes)   181

Charred Shrimp and Avocado Salad
(Time: 25 minutes)   183

Mixed Green and Herb Toss Salad
(Time: 10 minutes)   186

Chicken and Red Plum Salads
(Time: 20 minutes)   189

Chapter 5: Healthy Meat Recipes   **192**

Cheesy Meatball Skillet (Time: 30 minutes)   194

Swedish Meatballs (Time: 30 minutes)   197

Meatballs In Creamy Dill Sauce
(Time: 24 minutes)   200

Turkey Meatballs (Time: 30 minutes)   203

Steak Burritos (Time: 30 minutes)   206

Mustard-Maple Pork Tenderloin
(Time: 30 minutes)   209

Skillet Ravioli Lasagna (Time: 20 minutes)   212

Broccoli Beef (Time: 30 minutes)   215

Tenderloin Steak Diane (Time: 30 minutes)   218

Honey Garlic Pork Chops (Time: 22 minutes)   221

Greek Herbed Lamb (Time: 30 minutes)   224

Salisbury Steak with Mushroom Gravy
(Time: 30 minutes)   228

Chapter 6: Healthy Chicken Recipes   **233**

Potato and Chicken Sausage Hash Topped with Eggs
(Time: 30 minutes)   235

Mediterranean Chicken (Time: 25 minutes)   239

Chicken Stew (Time: 20 minutes)   242

Chicken Tikka Burritos (Time: 30 minutes)   245

Roast Chicken and Sweet Potatoes
(Time: 30 minutes)   248

Greek Cauliflower Rice Bowls with Grilled Chicken

(Time: 30 minutes)   251

Chapter 7: Healthy Dessert Recipes   254

Strawberry Lemon Shortcakes
(Time: 30 minutes)   256

Chocolate Chip Oatmeal Cookies
(Time: 20 minutes)   261

Apple Rings (Time: 25 minutes)   264

Rice Crispy Treat Bark (Time: 30 minutes)   267

S'mores Bars (Time: 30 minutes)   270

Meyer Lemon Cheesecake Shots
(Time: 20 minutes)   274

Chocolate Cake (Time: 30 minutes)   278

Glazed Apple Cinnamon Rolls

(Time: 30 minutes)   **283**

Conclusion   *288*

Other books by Gina Bates   *289*

Introduction

Here's a shocking dietary statistic: 320,000 of the total 700,000 deaths from cardiometabolic related illnesses in 2012 were as a result of the victims' poor diets (Micha, 2017). The foods you allow into your mouth do a lot more than satisfy your taste buds and placate your hunger. They are also a determining factor in the quality of life you will enjoy and how long you will remain alive. All of that may seem a tad too grim for you, but it is a fact of life we should not ignore or gloss over.

Understandably, the reason many people don't eat healthy foods is because of how busy modern life can get. The fees to enjoy even the most basic amenities keep traveling further north. We sleep for shorter periods than we did in past decades (Bin, et al, 2012), and this can be linked to urban life and the need to get ahead in a cutthroat world (Yetish, et al, 2015). This creates the necessity for a recipe book that contains healthy meals which can be prepared as quickly as possible: breakfasts you can whip up before running to work, and desserts you can make on the weekends and still have the time to kick you feet up and enjoy a book or your favorite TV show.

Fast Cooker Recipes is just that book for you. Everything you will need in order to achieve the desired look and taste for that meal is detailed out. As such, even if you do not consider yourself a good cook, this book is that helping hand you have always needed to create delicious, healthy, and quick meals.

Note that the nutritional information in this book is based on a diet of 2000 calories per day.

I am grateful if you would release reviews that will allow me to improve my work.

Chapter 1:

Healthy Breakfast

Recipes

Thank you for choosing this recipe book,

I hope it is useful for you.

I would like

have your own opinion on the recipes

you are going to prepare.

Your help will help me to improve

and deepen the arguments.

I thank you in advance if you want to help me
and enjoy your work.

Egg and Fried Rice Olé

(Time: 15 minutes)

Nutritional value per serving:

One serving contains:

- Total fats — 6 grams of monounsaturated fat, 3 grams of polyunsaturated fat, and 4 grams of saturated fat.

- 36 grams of total carbohydrates — 4 grams of total sugars and 6 grams of dietary fibre

- 436 milligrams of sodium

- 14 grams of protein

- 196 milligrams of cholesterol

- 327 calories

Total servings: 6

Utensils to use are:

- Wok or skillet — for cooking ingredients

- Spoon or spatula — To stir

- Bowl — To hold ingredients

- Knife and chopping board — To cut ingredients

- Colander — To rinse and drain the rice

Ingredients to use are:

- 6 eggs (fried)

- ¼ tsp of salt

- 3 cloves of garlic (minced)

- ¼ cup of grumbles Cotija cheese

- 1 tsp of chilli powder

- 1 cup of frozen corn (already thawed)

- 2 tbsp of canola oil

- ½ tsp of cumin (ground)

- ¼ cup of snipped, fresh cilantro

- ¼ cup of salsa verde

- 2 fresh poblano Chile peppers, seeded and cut up into bite size strips (medium-sized variety)

- 2 cups of chilled, cooked brown rice

- 1 can of pinto beans, rinsed and drained or 1 can of black beans (no-salt-added variety) (15 ounces)

- ¼ cup of red onion (finely chopped)

- 1 red sweet pepper, seeded and cut into bite-size strips (medium-sized variety)

Directions for preparation

1. Grab a large skillet or work and place on the cooker. Pour in 1 tbsp of oil to heat over medium heat.

2. Add the corn, sweet pepper, and poblano peppers to the heating oil and cook for 5 minutes until the ingredients begin to char. Stir occasionally with a spoon or spatula.

3. Pour in the garlic and cook for 30 seconds. Stir regularly.

4. Remove the mixture from the wok or skillet into a bowl and set aside.

5. Pour in the remaining 1 tbsp of oil into the skillet or wok. Pour in the rice and cook for 3 minutes while stirring occasionally until it dries and begins to crisp.

6. Add the cooked onions and peppers mix to the wok.

7. Proceed to add 1 tsp of chilli powder, ¼ tsp of salt to taste, 1 can of black beans (no-salt-added variety) or rinsed and drained pinto beans, ½ tsp of cumin (ground) and ¼ cup of snipped, fresh cilantro. Stir.

8. Leave to cook until thoroughly heated while stirring regularly.

9. Sprinkle each serving with cotija cheese, salsa verde, more fresh cilantro, and red onion. Top with one fried egg per serving.

Recipe Tips

• Chile peppers could be irritating on your eyes and skin as a result of the oils they contain, so endeavour to protect your skin by wearing rubber or plastic gloves before handling them.

• Rinse the chilled brown rice under running water and drain in a colander to remove excess starch. Spread the rice over paper towels and pat to dry.

How to make the Fried eggs

Ingredients to use are:

• Salt

• 6 eggs (large size)

• Black pepper

- 1 tbsp of butter or non-stick cooking spray

Directions for preparation

- Get an extra large skillet and place over a cooker. Coat the unheated skillet with non-stick cooking spray or melt 1 tbsp of butter over medium-high heat.

- Break all 6 eggs into the skillet one at a time.

- Sprinkle in the black pepper and salt to taste.

- Turn down the heat to low and cover the skillet to cook for 3 to 4 minutes until the yolks begin to harden and the egg whites are completely set.

- Use eggs to top each serving.

Recipe Tips

- If you prefer your eggs over easy, turn the eggs over to cook for an added 30 seconds after the yolks begins to thicken and the whites are completely set.

- If, however, you prefer over well eggs; flip over the eggs and cook for an added 1 minute.

Note:

Breakfast Tacos

(Time: 25 minutes)

Nutritional value per serving:

One serving (1 taco) contains:

- 10 grams of total fats — 4 grams of saturated fat

- 14 grams of protein

- 23 grams of total carbohydrates — 2 grams of total sugars and 3 grams of dietary fibre

- 44 milligrams of cholesterol

- 236 Calories

Total servings: 12

Utensils to use are:

- Oven — To heat the tortillas

- Oven racks — To hold the tortillas

- Foil (Tin or aluminium) — For wrapping the tortillas

- Baking sheet — To hold the foil wraps

- Skillet (large size) — For frying the filling

- Wooden spoon or heatproof spatula — For stirring

- Regular kitchen spoon (Large size) — For mashing

Ingredients to use are:

- Chorizo turkey sausage, ground (16 ounces)

- 1 small bunch of finely chopped green onions (divided)

- 12 small tortillas (flour variety)

- ½ cup of already made salsa; add extra for serving

- 1 tbsp of olive oil (extra-virgin) variety

- 1 can of black beans, rinsed and drained (low sodium variety) (15 ounces)

- 1 cup of freshly shredded, sharp Cheddar cheese (3 ounces)

Preferable garnishes:

- Fresh cilantro, finely chopped

- Avocado, peeled and sliced

- Regular tomatoes or grape tomatoes, washed and diced, or cherries, cut in halves

Directions for preparation

1. Begin by heating the tortillas. Place an oven rack into the oven and begin preheating the oven to a temperature of 350°F.

2. Divide the tortillas into two stacks comprising of 5 tortillas each. Proceed to wrap both stacks in foil.

3. Grab a baking sheet (ungreased) and place the stacks on it.

4. Place both stacks into the oven to heat for 8 to 10 minutes until they are thoroughly warmed. Retrieve the tortillas from the oven and set aside until you are ready to serve the tacos. Still leave the foil on.

5. Grab the skillet (large size) and place over medium heat. Pour in 1 tbsp of extra virgin olive oil.

6. Add the turkey sausage to the oil as it becomes hot, not smoking. Take caution and stand back quickly as the oil may splatter around.

7. Break the sausage into smaller pieces with a heatproof spatula or wooden spoon.

8. Cook for 8 minutes until the turkey sausage is fully cooked and begins to turn brown.

9. Pour in the salsa and black beans (low sodium variety). Stir the mixture to combine evenly.

10. Grab a large regular kitchen spoon and proceed to mash the black beans gently with the back.

11. Cover the skillet and cook for about 3 minutes until the salsa has given off its liquid and the beans are thoroughly cooked.

12. Add two-thirds of the finely chopped green onions while reserving some for serving. Stir the mixture and cook for another 30 seconds.

13. Turn down the heat and take off the filling.

14. Stuff and serve by unwrapping the warm tortillas and pouring about ⅓ cup of filling into each.

15. Top each taco with a generous amount of cheese or any other toppings of your choice. Garnish with any of the aforementioned garnishes.

Best enjoyed immediately.

Recipe tips:

- Swap flour tortillas for corn if you prefer gluten free tacos.

- When you go shopping, focus on getting ground turkey chorizo sausage. It is usually sold in bulk packages at meat markets.

- If you can't seem to get this type of ground turkey sausage, look for regular chorizo. However, it is important you understand that the regular chorizo and the Spanish cured chorizo are distinct chorizo types in themselves. The latter is already cooked and in slices like salami. Although delicious in its own sense, the Spanish cured chorizo will not fit into this recipe.

- You can prepare your filling beforehand, up to 1 day ahead. If you do this, all you need do is to heat the tortillas as directed in the 'directions for preparation' and reheat the filling before serving as tacos.

- In the case of leftovers, store in an airtight container and place in the refrigerator. Proceed to reheat and serve over rice or with scrambled eggs. You could even make more tacos.

Note:

Oven Denver Omelette

(Time: 30 minutes)

Nutritional value per serving

One serving contains:

- 4 grams of total carbohydrates — 0 grams of dietary fibre and 2 grams of total sugars

- 17 grams of protein

- 16 grams of total fats — 8 grams of saturated fat

- 506 milligrams of sodium

- 326 milligrams of cholesterol

- 235 calories

Total servings: 6

Utensils to use are:

- Bowl (large size)

- Whisk or large fork

- Baking dish/pan (9-inch square variety)

- Oven

Ingredients to use are:

- ¼ cup of finely chopped onions

- 8 eggs (large variety)

- 1 cup of fully cooked ham, finely chopped

- ½ cup of cream (half-and-half variety)

- 1 cup of Cheddar cheese, shredded

- ¼ cup of green pepper, finely chopped

Directions for preparation

1. Grab a large bowl. Break all 8 eggs into it and add cream. Beat the egg and cream mix with a whisk or large fork.

2. Add the finely chopped green pepper, onions, and ham, as well as the shredded cheese. Stir thoroughly.

3. Grab a baking dish or pan (9-inch square variety). Grease with butter or oil.

4. Put the pan into the oven and bake for 25 minutes at 400°F until the mix turns golden brown.

Recipe Tips:

- The type of pepper used in a typical Denver omelette is green pepper, but you can experiment with others like red, orange, and yellow for a burst of color.

- The puffed and golden brown style is the American style for this omelette. If you prefer your omelette less brown and more tender, bake it at a reduced temperature of about 325°F.

- Use a thermometer to measure your progress. Once it reads 160°F, the eggs are set.

Note:

Poached Egg and Beans

(Time: 15 minutes)

Nutritional value per serving

One serving contains:

- Total fats — 4 grams of monounsaturated fat, 2 grams of polyunsaturated fat, and 2 grams of saturated fat

- 469 milligrams of sodium

- 16 grams of protein

- 24 grams of total carbohydrates — 4 grams of total sugars and 8 grams of dietary fibre.

- 186 milligrams of cholesterol

- 219 calories

Total servings: 4

Utensils to use are:

- Skillet (large variety) — To cook the ingredients

- Slotted spoon — To drain eggs

- Custard cup — To hold eggs

- Bowls — To hold ingredients

Ingredients to use are:

- ¼ cups of green onions, freshly chopped (based on preference)

- 2 cups of fresh button mushrooms (sliced)

- 2 tsp of olive oil

- 4 cups of fresh spinach or kale (chopped)

- 4 large eggs

- ¼ tsp of salt (garlic salt variety)

- 1 cup of grape tomatoes cut into quarters or ½ cup of oil-packed dried tomatoes, sliced

- 1 tbsp of cider vinegar

- ¼ tsp of pepper (black or lemon-pepper variety)

- 1 can of cannellini beans (white kidney beans), rinsed and drained (15 ounces)

1.Grab a large skillet and place on a cooker. Pour in 4 cups of water.

2. Add vinegar to the water and allow to simmer.

3. Proceed to break an egg into the custard cup. Pour the egg into the simmering water. Repeat the process with the other eggs. Allow each egg the same amount of space.

4. Cook for 3 to 5 minutes until the yolks begin to thicken but isn't hard, and the egg whites set completely.

5. Take out the eggs and put them into a bowl with a slotted spoon. Keep warm.

6. Empty out the skillet and wipe it clean before replacing it on the cooker over medium heat.

7. Pour 2 tsp of olive oil into the skillet to heat and add mushrooms. Cook for about 3 to 5 minutes until mushrooms become tender. Stir regularly.

8. Add the kale and cook for 30 seconds until it becomes wilted. Stir regularly.

9. Proceed to stir in the salt, lemon-pepper seasoning, and beans. Leave to cook.

10. Divide the beans mixture into bowls and top with one poached egg each and freshly chopped green onions if preferred.

Preferable Garnishes:

You can choose to garnish your poached egg and beans with any of the following garnishes.

Italian:

Serve meals with fresh basil (snipped), finely chopped prosciutto, a drizzle of balsamic vinegar (optional) and Parmesan cheese (shredded).

Mexican:

Serve with plain yogurt (low-fat variety), queso fresco, snipped fresh cilantro (optional), and salsa verde.

Southern:

Serve with sour cream (light variety), bottled, hot pepper sauce (optional), and cheddar cheese, shredded.

Mediterranean:

Serve with snipped fresh oregano (optional), crumbled feta cheese, and plain yogurt (low-fat variety).

Asian:

Serve with sriracha sauce, toasted sesame oil (optional), soy sauce, and kimchi.

Note:

_____

_____

_____

_____

_____

Tofu Stir Fry

(Time: 25 minutes)

Nutritional value per serving

One serving contains:

- 17 grams of total fats — 2 grams of saturated fat

- 22 grams of protein

- 12 grams of total carbohydrates — 1 gram of total sugars, and 5 grams of dietary fibre.

- 297 calories

Total servings: 3 to 4

Utensils to use are:

- Colander — To rinse and drain the tofu

- Paper towels — To dry the tofu

- Wok or skillet (non-stick variety) — For cooking the ingredients

- Knife and chopping board — To chop the tofu

- Spoon — For stirring

Ingredients to use are:

- 2 tsp of sesame oil

- 1 tbsp of grapeseed oil or canola oil

- Baby spinach (10 ounces)

- 1 tbsp of fresh ginger, minced

- 2 tbsp of toasted sesame seeds

- 3 large cloves of garlic, minced (roughly 1 tbsp)

- 3 tbsp of soy sauce (low-sodium variety), divided, with extra to taste

- 2 packets of tofu (extra-firm variety)

- 1 to 2 tsp of fresh chili paste (sambal oelek) or ¼ to ½ tsp of red pepper flakes

- 1 small bunch of green onions, finely chopped and divided

Directions for preparation

1. Place the tofu in a colander and rinse under running water. Drain out excess water.

2.Grab some paper towels and proceed to wrap every block of tofu in a double layer. Pat to dry while pressing down on the tofu to squeeze out any excess moisture.

3.Place the tofu on a chopping board and cut it up into cubes of ¾ inches.

4.Get a wok or skillet (non-stick variety) and place over medium heat. Pour in 1 tbsp of canola oil to heat.

5.Add the tofu to the oil once it becomes hot but not smoking. Take caution in adding the tofu as the oil will splatter a bit.

6.Add 1 tbsp of soy sauce. Sauté for 8 to 10 minutes, and stir regularly until the tofu has given off all its moisture and attains a nice shade on all sides. You don't have to stir constantly at this stage. Allow the tofu sit on its sides for a while to achieve perfect browning.

7.Add the remaining 2 tbsp of soy sauce, garlic, ginger, two-thirds of the chopped green onions, and chili paste. Cook for 1 minute, stirring regularly until the sauce becomes fragrant.

8.   Proceed to add several large handfuls of baby spinach. Stir in the baby spinach so that it wilts

and allows more space to add more. Once the baby spinach completely wilts, proceed to add more by the handful. Repeat the stirring process to wilt the additional baby spinach. Although the amount of baby spinach might seem ridiculous at the beginning, over time, it will wilt and cook down.

9. Add the sesame seeds and 2 tsp of sesame oil. Stir to blend in, and allow to cook for 30 seconds.

10. Turn off the heat. Sprinkle the remaining chopped green onions over the top.

11. Serve hot with noodles, rice (brown), or any other serving of your choice. Add a few drizzles of soy sauce and flakes or chili paste to alter the taste to your preference.

Servings:

The tofu stir fries can be served with:

- Quinoa

- Rice (cauliflower variety)

- Rice noodles or soba

- Brown rice

- For your tofu, do not use any other variety (silken, firm, etcetera) other than extra-firm for this recipe.

- Baby spinach can be replaced with any variety of spinach you prefer. The reason baby spinach is preferred in this recipe is because it cooks quickly; this is why it is sautéed with the tofu in the pan.

- Olive oil isn't recommended for this stir fry recipe because of the high level of heat involved. Olive oil has a lower smoke point. As such, it can easily cause your ingredients to start burning, which will affect the overall flavor and taste of the dish.

- When adding other veggies such as peppers or broccoli, it is advisable to cook the tofu in adherence to the recipe's directions from step 5, before removing it to a plate when it is browned.

- If you like, you can also add other spices such as ginger and garlic to the pan filled with vegetables of your choice. Ensure you add some more oil, though.

- Cook the vegetables for about 5 to 8 minutes until they become crisp and tender. Proceed to add the tofu back and continue with the directions of the recipe.

- You can refrigerate or freeze any leftovers for up to 5 days. However, it's imperative you know that the vegetables could become slightly mushy and a tad soft when frozen.

Note:

Avocado Toast with Egg

(Time: 10 minutes)

Nutritional value per serving

One serving contains:

- 11.9 grams of protein

- 22.9 grams of fat - 5 grams of saturated fat

- 20.8 grams of carbohydrates - 8.8 grams of fiber

- 361 milligrams of sodium

- 3 grams of sugar

- 4 milligrams of iron

- 191 milligrams of cholesterol

- 321 calories

Total servings: 2

Utensils to use are:

- 1 small skillet, of the nonstick variety

- 1 small bowl

- 1 toaster

- 1 mini avocado masher

Ingredients to use are:

- 1 tsp of butter

- 2 large eggs

- 1 small peeled avocado with the pits removed, and mashed

- 2 slices of wholegrain bread

- A single pinch of cayenne pepper

- Black pepper and kosher salt to taste

- Lemon juice to taste

Directions for preparation

1. Set the heat on your stove to medium-low and place your skillet over it.

2. Melt your butter in the skillet and crack your eggs into oil. Do not place the eggs on top of each

other. One egg should be beside the next. Once the bottom of the eggs are firm enough, flip them carefully (you should try to keep the yolk intact. Don't beat yourself up about it if the yolk cracks). This should take about 5 minutes before your egg is done.

3. While the eggs cook, toast your wholegrain bread for about 4 minutes.

4. Put the mashed avocado in a bowl. Add cayenne pepper, kosher salt, and lemon juice. Stir the mixture well.

5. Place some of the avocado mixture onto a slice of toasted bread. Put the egg on the top of that avocado mixture and sprinkle some black pepper on it.

Note:

Southwestern Waffles

(Time:13 minutes)

Nutritional value per serving

One serving contains:

- 738 milligrams of sodium

- 5.7 grams of protein

- 31.8 grams of carbohydrates - 1.4 grams of fiber

- 8.5 grams of fat - 5 grams of saturated fat

- 57 milligrams of cholesterol

- 7 grams of sugar

- 2 milligrams iron

- Vitamin C 22mg

- 207 calories

Total servings: 10

Utensils to use are:

- 1 waffle iron

- 1 large bowl

- 1 chopping board

- 1 small kitchen knife

Ingredients to use are:

- 2 large eggs (the egg whites)

- 1 cup of milk

- ⅓ cup of melted butter

- 2 tbsp of honey

- 1 cup of all purpose flour

- 4 tsp of baking powder

- ⅓ cup of yellow or white cornmeal

- ½ cup corn

- 2 tsp of sea salt

- 2 green chile peppers with all its seeds removed and diced

Directions for preparation

1. Heat up your waffle iron.

2. Whisk the egg whites in a bowl before adding honey, butter, and milk. Whisk this mixture well. Stir baking powder, cornmeal, and flour into and mix, then add your sea salt. Also, add corn and green chiles and continue to stir until the mixture attains a smooth appearance.

3. Take some of that mixture and place it in your waffle iron. Close the iron and cook until it no longer steams. Do the same for all the mixture left in the bowl. The batter may take about 4 minutes to be crispy and ready.

Note:

Savory Oatmeal with Cheddar and Fried Eggs

(Time: 10 minutes)

Nutritional value per serving

One serving contains:

- 13 grams of protein

- 3 grams of sugar

- 18 grams of carbohydrates - 3 grams of fiber

- 16 grams of fat - 9 grams of saturated fat

- 201 milligrams of cholesterol

- 178 milligrams of sodium

- 262 calories

Total servings: 1

Utensils to use are:

- 1 small pan of the nonstick kind

- 1 pot (preferably a ceramic cooking pot)

- 1 small kitchen knife

- 1 chopping board

- 1 small grater

Ingredients to use are:

- 1 large egg

- ¼ cup of steel cut oats

- 1 cup of water

- 2 tbsp of cheddar cheese, which has been shredded

- 1 tsp of coconut oil

- Half an onion, finely diced

- ¼ finely chopped red peppers

- Salt and pepper to desired taste

Directions for preparation

1. Set your stove to medium-high heat and place a pot of water on it. When it starts boiling, add your oatmeal and reduce the heat to medium-low. Cook the oatmeal until you can no longer observe water in the pot. This should take about 4 to 5 minutes.

Turn the heat off and add your shredded cheese to the oatmeal. Also, add salt and pepper to taste and stir the mixture well.

2. Set your stove to medium-high heat and place your nonstick pan on it. Add half of the coconut oil into the pan. Add your finely chopped red peppers and cook until they are soft and done. Take them out and place them on your oatmeal.

3. Add what is left of your coconut oil onto your pan. Set the stove to medium-low and fry your eggs sunny side up.

4. Place it on your oatmeal, and will be ready to be eaten. If you prefer, chop some walnuts and add them to the oatmeal.

Note:

Zucchini Bread Oatmeal

(Time: 13 minutes)

Nutritional value per serving

One serving contains:

- 7 grams of protein

- 54 grams of carbohydrates - 10 grams of fiber

- 17 grams of fat - 9 grams of saturated fat

- 14 grams of sugar

- 220 milligrams of sodium

- 380 calories

Total servings: 2

Utensils to use are:

- 1 blender

- 1 grater

- 1 medium ceramic cooking pot

- 1 small bowl

- 1 vegetable peeler

Ingredients to use are:

- 1 cup of coconut milk

- ⅔ cup of rolled oats

- 1 cup of grated zucchinis

- 2 tbsp of chia seeds

- A pinch of sea salt

- Half a tablespoon of mashed ripe bananas

- ¼ tsp of nutmeg, freshly grated

- 1 tsp of vanilla extract

- Cinnamon to desired taste

- Dark chocolate shavings

Directions for preparation

1. Put your oatmeal, grated zucchinis, chia seeds, mashed bananas, grated nutmeg, and cinnamon into a pot. Add the coconut milk and stir the mixture over medium-high heat until it thickens. This may take up to 9 minutes for all the liquid to

be completely absorbed. Add salt to your desired taste at this point.

2. Turn off the heat and stir the vanilla extract into the mixture.

3. Top it with the chocolate shavings and enjoy.

Note:

Skinny Spiced Coconut Yogurt Quinoa Muffins

(Time: 30 minutes)

Nutritional value per serving

One serving contains:

- 4 grams of protein

- 5 grams of fat

- 29 grams of carbohydrates - 2 grams of fiber

- 11 grams of sugar

- 72 milligrams of sodium

- 209 milligrams of potassium

- 175 calories

Total servings: 10

Utensils to use are:

- 1 blender

- 1 muffin tin with 12 cups

- 2 medium bowls

Ingredients to use are:

- 1 tbsp of whole ground flaxseed meal

- ¼ tsp of salt

- 3 tbsp of water

- Half a cup of mashed bananas

- Half a tsp of vanilla bean powder

- 1 tsp of ground nutmeg

- Half a cup of unsweetened applesauce

- 1 tsp of cinnamon

- Half a cup of coconut yogurt

- 2 tsp of baking powder

- ¼ of pure maple syrup

- ¼ cup of granulated coconut sugar

- 1 cup of ground oat flour

- Half a cup of blanched whole almond flour

- Half a cup of quinoa flakes

Directions for preparation

1. Make sure to preheat your oven to 350°F, then grease a muffin tin.

2. Put some flax in a bowl and add water to it. Leave it to gel.

3. Get a bowl and whisk your mashed bananas, yogurt, applesauce, and maple syrup together. Add the flax to this mixture, and continue whisking for about a minute. Then, set it aside.

4. Get a different bowl and put your vanilla bean powder, ground nutmeg, cinnamon, baking powder, coconut sugar, oat flour, almond flour, and quinoa flakes into it. Add some salt and mix them together.

5. Combine this mixture into the earlier banana mixture, and stir it until the mixture thickens.

6. Partially fill (about ¾ of it) some cups of your muffin tin with the batter. Put some water in the unused ones. Add some quinoa flakes to the batter and, using the center rack of your oven, bake for about 24 minutes.

7.You should let it cool down before taking out the muffins.

Note:

_____

_____

_____

_____

_____

_____

Egg In a Nest

(Time: 10 minutes)

Nutritional value per serving

One serving contains:

- 9.41 grams of protein

- 14.33 grams of carbohydrates - 1.2 grams of fiber

- 11.44 grams of fat - 5.43 grams of saturated fat

- 1.87 grams of sugar

- 201.27 milligrams of cholesterol

- 215.85 milligrams of sodium

- 199 calories

Total servings: 2

Utensils to use are:

- 1 small kitchen knife

- 1 large skillet of the nonstick variety

- 1 flat spatula

Ingredients to use are:

- 2 slices of bread

- Ground black pepper

- 1 tbsp of butter, unsalted

- 2 large eggs

- Salt to desired taste

Directions for preparation

1. Cut a small hole at the center of each of the bread slices.

2. Set your stove to medium heat and place your skillet over it. Melt your unsalted butter into the skillet and, when it starts to foam, place your bread slices. Open an egg into the holes in each of the slices of bread, and add salt and pepper. Flip until both sides have been browned. This may take up to 6 minutes. Be careful not to burn the bread or egg.

Note:

Fast Hammy Grits

(Time: 15 minutes)

Nutritional value per serving

One serving contains:

- 15.63 grams of protein

- 25.8 grams of carbohydrates - 1.46 grams of fiber

- 25.39 grams of fat - 11.64 grams of saturated fat

- 3.49 grams of sugar

- 67.01 milligrams of cholesterol

- 655.21 milligrams of sodium

- 395 calories

Total servings: 2

Utensils to use are:

- 1 chopping board

- 1 small kitchen knife

- 1 small saucepan

- 1 medium skillet

- 1 large box grater

- 2 medium bowls

Ingredients to use are:

- 1 cup of water

- 1 hot sauce

- Half a cup of whole milk

- 1 medium sized scallion

- 1 tbsp of butter, unsalted kind

- ¼ cup of cheddar cheese

- 2 tsp of vegetable oil

- ⅓ cup of boiled cornmeal, whether yellow or white

- Half a cup of finely chopped cooked ham, about 57 grams (1 oz)

- Ground black pepper and kosher salt to taste

1. Set your stove to medium-high heat and place a saucepan on it. Put some milk, butter, and water into the pan. Also, add salt and pepper and let the contents of the saucepan simmer for a bit.

2. While that is simmering, set another burner to medium-high heat and place a skillet containing vegetable oil on it. When the oil begins to simmer, put your diced ham into the skillet and stir for about 5 minutes. Make sure all sides of each ham is brown before putting the stove off.

3. Pour your boiled cornmeal into your simmering milk and butter mixture and whisk. After a minute, stop stirring and leave them to boil for another minute.

4. Now, turn off the stove and cover the pot with a lid. Set it aside for about 6 minutes.

5. Next, shred your cheddar cheese into a cup and slice your scallion (the light green and white parts).

6. Uncover your boiled cornmeal and stir until the contents are smooth. Add some cheese to the grits and stir them well together, until the cheese melts. Add salt and pepper to your taste.

7. This can now be emptied into two medium bowls. Sprinkle some more cheese, ham, and scallion onto each of the bowls. You may dab some hot sauce on them if you like.

Note:

Breakfast Nachos

(Time: 25 minutes)

Nutritional value per serving

One serving contains:

- 26.8 grams of protein

- 31.8 grams of carbohydrates - 2.9 grams of fiber

- 1 gram of sugar

- 57.4 grams of fat - 21.7 grams of saturated fat

- 239 milligrams of cholesterol

- 1272 milligrams of sodium

- 154 milligrams of calcium

- 3 milligrams of iron

- 11 milligrams of vitamin C

- 744 calories

Total servings: 10

Utensils to use are:

- 1 medium skillet

- 1 medium grater

Ingredients to use are:

- ¼ tsp of dried oregano or a pinch

- 2 tsp of butter

- 1 shredded slice of cheddar cheese

- 2 large eggs

- Two ¾ filled cups of potato chips

- 4 oz of beef chorizo (¼ pounds)

- Salt and pepper (cayenne) to taste

Directions for preparation

1. Place your skillet on a stove that has been set to medium heat. Melt some butter into it and break your eggs into the skillet. Fry the egg for about 2 minutes (before the eggs turn brown and after the whites become opaque). Add salt and pepper to your desired taste and flip until both sides are done.

2. Set the stove to medium-high heat and brown your chorizo in the skillet. This should take no more than 10 minutes.

3. Now, to serve breakfast. Put your eggs and potato chips on a plate. Put some beef chorizo on them and sprinkle with cheese and oregano.

Note:

Hootsla (egg bread)

(Time: 10 minutes)

Nutritional value per serving

One serving contains:

- 15.3 grams of protein

- 39.7 grams of carbohydrates - 1.56 grams of fiber

- 5.52 grams of sugar

- 19.31 grams of fat - 9.99 grams of saturated fat

- 516.47 milligrams of sodium

- 220.6 milligrams of cholesterol

- 391 calories

Total servings: 8

Utensils to use are:

- 1 chopping board

- 1 small kitchen knife

- 1 balloon whisk

- 1 large skillet

- 1 medium sized bowl

Ingredients to use are:

- 6 large eggs

- Maple syrup

- A sweet baguette, cut into little cubes to fill 8 small cups (preferably a day old)

- 1 cup of whole milk

- 6 tbsp of butter, unsalted

- Salt to desired taste

Directions for preparation

1. Break eggs open into a bowl, add milk and salt to it, and whisk the mixture.

2. Place a skillet over medium-high heat and melt some butter into the pan till it foams. Place your baguette cubes into the hot oil and fry the bread until all the sides appear toasted (brown in color).

3. Turn off the heat and pour your egg and milk mixture on the bread cubes. Make sure every side

of the bread is coated with the mixture before turning the heat back on. When the egg is cooked, your Hootsla is ready to be served.

4. Some maple syrup would make this meal even more delicious.

Note:

Banana and Fromage Blanc Grilled Cheese

(Time: 15 minutes)

Nutritional value per serving

One serving contains:

- 9.6 grams of protein

- 46.75 grams of carbohydrates - 3.9 grams of fiber

- 17.34 grams of fat - 9.82 grams of saturated fat

- 8.56 grams of sugar

- 37.71 milligrams of cholesterol

- 276.93 milligrams of sodium

- 371 calories

Total servings: 1

Utensils to use are:

- 1 small knife

- 1 chopping board

- 1 small bowl

- 1 large skillet

Ingredients to use are:

- 3 tbsp of fromage blanc cheese

- 2 slices of cinnamon-raisin bread, half an inch thick

- Half a medium banana that has been chopped into small pieces

- 1 tbsp of softened, unsalted butter

- ¼ tsp of vanilla extract

- Powdered sugar as desired

Directions for preparation

1. Mix your vanilla, fromage blanc, banana, and sugar in a small bowl.

2. Heat a skillet over medium heat and coat your cinnamon-raisin bread slices with butter.

3. With the buttered side of the slices facing up, place them on your skillet. Also, spread your vanilla mixture on the bread and cover it with the

second slice (this should also have its buttered side up).

4. Flip the bread to make sure both sides are equally toasted. This should take up to 8 minutes (4 minutes for both sides).

Note:

Chapter 2:

Healthy Appetizer

Recipes

Thank you for choosing this recipe book,
I hope it is useful for you.

         ,

I would like

have your own opinion on the recipes

you are going to prepare.

Your help will help me to improve

and deepen the arguments.

I thank you in advance if you want to help me
and enjoy your work.

Pastrami Roll-ups

(Time: 15 minutes)

Nutritional value per serving

One serving contains:

- 0 grams of total carbohydrates — 0 gram of dietary fibre and 0 gram of total sugars

- 2 grams of total fats — 1 gram of saturated fat

- 2 grams of protein

- 158 milligrams of sodium

- 8 kilogram of cholesterol

- 25 calories

Total servings: 4 dozens (48 roll-ups)

Utensils to use are:

- Bowl (small size) — To mix ingredients

- Whisk — To blend ingredients

- Paper towels — For drying ingredients

- Knife — To apply spread and cut up pastrami rolls

Ingredients to use are:

- 12 dill pickle spears

- ¾ cups of cream cheese (spreadable variety)

- 12 slices of lean deli pastrami

- ½ cup of crumbled cheese (blue variety)

Directions for preparation

1. Get a small bowl and pour in the blue cheese and cream cheese. Beat with the whisk until a well blended mix is achieved.

2. Get some paper towels and pat dry the pickles and pastrami, if wet.

3. Use a knife to spread the blue and cream cheese mix (roughly 1 tbsp) over every slice of pastrami.

4. Top each cheese mix spread on a pastrami with a pickle spear, and tightly roll up the pastrami.

5. Use the knife to cut up each roll of pastrami into 4 slices or more, depending on the size of your preference.

6. Refrigerate any leftovers.

Note:

Poached Shrimp

(Time: 30 minutes)

Nutritional value per serving

One serving contains:

- 3 grams of total fats — 1 gram of saturated fat

- 39 gram of protein

- 3 grams of total carbohydrates — 0 gram of total sugars, and 0 gram of dietary fibre

- 1610 milligrams of sodium

- 360 milligrams of cholesterol

- 200 calories

Total servings: 4

Utensils to use are:

- Kitchen shears — To devein shrimp

- Stockpot — To cook ingredients

- Bowl — To hold the shrimp

- Slotted spoon — For draining the shrimp

- Colander — To drain the shrimp

Ingredients to use:

- 1 bay leaf

- 2 lemons (both cut in half)

- Salt (Kosher variety)

- 1 celery stalk

- 1 cup of dry white wine

- 1 onion (cut into quarters)

- ½ bunch of fresh parsley (flat-leaf variety)

- 1½ pounds of large shrimp (fresh with the shell on)

- 1 tbsp of peppercorns (black variety)

Serving:

- Eat with lemon wedges and cocktail sauce.

Direction for preparation

1. Grab a pair of kitchen shears and cut into the shrimps. Guide the blade along the length of the

shells covering the shrimp's backs. Be careful that the shears just cut deep enough into the flesh to uncover the veins. Take out the veins.

2. Place your stockpot over the cooker and pour in some water to boil. Sprinkle in a generous amount of salt.

3. Add the bay leaf, the chopped onion, 1 tbsp of black peppercorns, ½ bunch of parsley (flat-leaf variety), and 1 celery stalk. Top with 1 cup of dry white wine.

4. Proceed to squeeze in the juice from the halved lemons into the stockpot before adding the lemons.

5. Turn down the volume of the heat and cover to cook for 10 to 15 minutes. Afterwards, proceed to turn up the heat.

6. Pour in the deveined shrimps and cover to cook while turning off the heat completely.

7. Allow to sit for 3 minutes until the shrimp are completely cooked.

8. Get a slotted spoon and drain out the shrimp into a bowl filled with ice water. Let sit to cool.

9. Drain the shrimp with a colander and proceed to peel off the shell while leaving the tails in place.

10. Best served with lemon wedges and cocktail sauce.

Note:

Tuna Lettuce Wraps

(Time: 10 minutes)

Nutritional value per serving

One serving contains:

- 17 grams of total fats — 3 grams of saturated fat

- 40 grams of protein

- 0.6 gram of salt

- 8 grams of total carbohydrates — 8 grams of dietary fibre, and 7 grams of sugars

- 361 calories

Total servings: 2

Utensils to use are:

- Kitchen brush — To oil the tuna

- Pan (non-stick variety) — To cook the tuna

- Plate — To hold ingredients

- Spoon — For scooping avocado flesh, and mashing

- Spatula — For moving the tuna

- Serving plates — To lay out the dish

- Knife — For cutting ingredients

Ingredients to use are:

- 1 avocado (ripened)

- ½ tsp of mustard powder (English variety)

- 2 drops of rapeseed oil (for brushing the tuna)

- 1 tbsp of capers

- Defrosted, fresh tuna fillets (140 kilogram packets × 2)

- 8 lettuce leaves (romaine variety)

- 1 tsp of cider vinegar

- 16 cherry tomatoes, preferably still on the vine, cut into halves

Directions for preparation

1. Grab a cooking brush and proceed to brush up the tuna with 2 drops of rapeseed oil.

2. Put a non-stick pan over the cooker and drop the tuna in it to cook. Allow to cook on each side for about 1 minute. You can cook for longer if you like your fillet thicker.

3.Use a spatula to move the tuna from the pot onto a plate, and allow to sit and cool.

4. Get a knife and cut the avocado in half. Remove the core with a spoon and proceed to spoon out the edible flesh.

5. Put the flesh into a small bowl and sprinkle with ½ tsp of mustard powder (English variety).

6. Drizzle with 1 tsp of cider vinegar, and proceed to mash the mixture with a spoon until a smooth paste like mayonnaise is formed.

7. Add 1 tbsp of capers and stir thoroughly.

8. Spoon the mixture into 2 small dishes and place on the serving plates holding the sliced tomatoes and lettuce leaves.

9. Proceed to cut up the tuna. The insides should be a slight shade of pink. Arrange the slices of tuna on the serving plates.

10. Spoon some of the avocado serving sauce onto the lettuce leaves. Top with slices of cherry tomatoes and some slices of tuna.

11. Add a few extra helpings of capers if you want.

12. Roll up the lettuce leaves into wraps and serve.

Note:

Fig Toasties

(Time: 10 minutes)

Nutritional value per serving

One serving contains:

- 610 milligrams of sodium

- 15 grams of total fats — 8 grams of saturated fat

- 12 grams of protein

- 34 grams of total carbohydrates — 5 grams of total sugars, and 2 grams of dietary fibre

- 40 milligrams of cholesterol

- 320 calories

Total servings: 8

Utensils to use are:

- Oven — For baking the toasties

- Bowl (small size) — To mix the ingredients

- Skillet (large size) — For cooking the ingredients

- Knife — To apply the spread, and cut bread into shapes

- Spatula — For pressing down on sandwiches

- Wire rack — To hold ingredients as they bake

- Baking sheet — To hold ingredients on the rack.

Ingredients to use are:

- Salt (kosher variety)

- Grated cheddar (sharp white variety) (8 ounces)

- 1 tbsp of pepper flakes, crushed (red variety)

- ½ cup of fig jam

- 3 tbsp of room-temperature butter (unsalted variety)

- Sandwich bread, 12 slices (white variety)

- 1 tbsp of vinegar (red wine variety)

Directions for preparation

1. Begin by preheating the oven to a temperature of 250°F.

2. Get a bowl and pour in 1 tbsp of red wine vinegar and ½ cup of fig jam. Sprinkle with 1 tbsp of pepper flakes and work into a smooth, well-blended mix. Add salt to taste.

3. Spoon out half of the spicy fig jam mix and set aside.

4. Get 6 of the 12 slices of white sandwich bread. Apply the remaining half of the spicy fig jam mix as spread on the 6 slices.

5. Sprinkle the already spread bread with grated cheddar. Add the other 6 slices remaining to top off the spread in sandwich fashion.

6. Proceed to spread butter on the upper parts of the sandwiches.

7. Get a large-sized skillet and place over medium high heat. Cook the sandwiches in batches of two by firmly pressing down on them with a spatula. Subsequently, the cheese will melt and the part on the skillet will turn golden brown. Cook each side for about 1 minute. Set aside and repeat the process for the other sandwiches.

8. Get a wire rack used for baking and set it in the oven. Line the rack with a baking sheet and

proceed to transfer the sandwiches into the oven to warm slowly until you are ready to serve.

9. Cut all the sandwiches diagonally with a knife to form sandwich triangles.

10. Eat with the previously set aside spicy fig jam mix as dip.

Note:

Chickpea and Red Pepper Dip

(Time: 5 minutes)

Nutritional value per serving

One serving contains:

- 18 grams of total fats — 2 grams of saturated fat

- 5 grams of protein

- 12 grams of total carbohydrates — 2 grams of dietary fibre, and 0 gram total sugars

- 0.9 grams of salt

- 223 calories

Total servings: 4

Utensils to use are:

- Food processor — To make the dip

- Bowl — To serve the dip

Ingredients to use are:

- 2 red peppers, deseeded, roasted and chopped

- 1 clove of garlic, crushed

- 1 small handful of fresh coriander, chopped

- 4 tbsp of olive oil (extra-virgin variety)

- Lemon juice, squeezed

- 1 can of rinsed and drained chickpeas (390 grams)

- Bread, toasted (pita variety)

Directions for preparation

1. Get a food processor and pour in 1 can of chickpeas, 2 deseeded, roasted and chopped red peppers, 1 crushed clove of garlic, 1 small handful of chopped coriander, and 4 tbsp of extra-virgin olive oil.

2. Drizzle with squeezed lemon juice before proceeding to turn on the food processor and purée the ingredients into a smooth paste.

3. Season with a sprinkle of salt to taste.

4. Scoop into a bowl and serve as a dip for toasted pita bread.

Note:

Wild Salmon and Avocado Triangles

(Time: 8 to 10 minutes)

Nutritional value per serving

One serving contains:

- 34 grams of total carbohydrates — 7 grams of dietary fibre, and 4 grams of total sugars

- 27 grams of total fats — 6 grams of saturated fat

- 44 grams of protein

- 0.8 gram of salt

- 572 calories

Total servings: 2

Utensils to use are:

- Pan — To cook ingredients

- Slotted spoon — To drain fish

- Knife and chopping board — To cut ingredients

- Bowl — For holding ingredients

- Spoon — To scoop out avocado

Ingredients to use are:

- 1 avocado (small size)

- 1 small-sized red onion, halved — one half finely chopped, the other sliced

- 1 lemon, cut in half

- 2 wild salmon fillets (skinless and boneless variety)

- A few dill sprigs, with extra to serve

- 3 bread slices, triangular-shaped

Directions for preparation

1. Place a pan over the cooker and pour in some water to boil. Squeeze in a generous amount of lemon juice, and add the sliced half of the red onion as well as a few dill sprigs.

2. Add the 2 salmon fillets, and let cook for about 8 to 10 minutes until it becomes easy to flake. Move the fish from the pan into a bowl using a slotted spoon, and flake into bits.

3. Cut up the avocado and remove the core. Using a spoon, scoop out the edible flesh into a bowl and drizzle with a generous amount of squeezed lemon juice. Proceed to mash into a smooth paste.

4. Get the 3 bread triangles and cut them in half. Place the cut side to face up, and spread with the avocado mash.

5. Sprinkle with the chopped half of the red onion, and some snipped dill. Add the flaked salmon and some more onions, if desired. Drizzle with some squeezed lemon juice and serve.

Note:

Peanut Hummus with Fruit and Veggie Sticks

(Time: 10 minutes)

Nutritional value per serving

One serving contains:

- 16 grams of total fats — 2 grams of saturated fat

- 15 grams of protein

- 35 grams of total carbohydrates — 13 grams of fibre, and 16 grams of sugar

- 0.8 gram of salt

- 336 calories

Total servings: 2

Utensils to use are:

- Knife and chopping board — To cut ingredients

- Food processor — For blitzing ingredients

- Bowl — To hold ingredients

Ingredients to use are:

- 1 tsp of oil (rapeseed variety)

- 1 tbsp of tahini

- 4 sticks of celery — cut into batons lengthwise

- 1 lemon, cut in half and zested (squeeze one half over apples to prevent browning)

- 2 carrots — cut into sticks

- 1 can of chickpeas (380 grams)

- ½ to 1 tsp of paprika (smoked variety)

- 2 tbsp of peanuts (roasted and unsalted variety)

- 2 crisp, red apples — remove core and slice

Directions for preparation

1. Rinse and drain the chickpeas while reserving their liquid. Measure out three-quarters of the chickpeas and put into a bowl.

2. Get a food processor and pour in the ¾ chickpeas. Add in the lemon zest, 1 tsp of paprika, 1 tbsp of tahini, 1 tsp of rapeseed oil, 2 tbsp of

roasted and unsalted peanuts, 3 tbsp of chickpea liquid, and a drizzle of lemon juice.

3. Proceed to turn on the food processor and blitz the ingredients until a smooth paste is formed.

4. Add the remaining chickpeas and stir thoroughly. Serve with veggies and fruit sticks.

Note:

Buckeye Balls

(Time: 30 minutes)

Nutritional value per servings

One serving contains:

- 170 grams of total fats — 3 grams of saturated fat

- 6 grams of total carbohydrates — 3 grams of total sugars and 3 grams of dietary fibre

- 120 milligrams of sodium

- 14 grams of protein

- 5 milligrams of cholesterol

- 170 calories

Total Servings: 25 balls

Utensils to use are:

- Bowl (medium-sized variety) — For mixing the ingredients

- Whisk — To beat the ingredients

- Stand mixer — To mix the ingredients

- Cookie sheet — To hold the cookies

- Parchment paper — To line the cookie sheet

- Cookie scoop — To cut the dough into portions

Ingredients to use are:

- 1 tsp of vanilla extract

- 1 tsp of salt

- 1 cup of unflavoured casein protein powder (100 grams)

- ½ cup of natural peanut butter (128 grams)

- 70% cacao dark chocolate, melted (4 ounces)

- ¾ cup of peanut flour (90 grams)

- 1½ tsp of liquid stevia extract

- 1½ cups of unsweetened vanilla almond milk

Directions for preparation

1. Get a bowl (medium-sized variety) and pour in the ¾ cup of peanut flour and 1 cup of protein

powder. Sprinkle with salt to taste, and beat with a whisk.

2. Get a stand mixer with an attached beater and fill its bowl with 1½ cups of unsweetened vanilla almond milk and ½ cup of natural peanut butter. Drizzle in 1½ tsp of liquid stevia extract and 1 tsp of vanilla extract. Run the beater on low speed to mix the ingredients thoroughly until smooth.

3. Add the dry ingredients (protein powder and peanut flour mix) to the bowl and mix until the ingredients are thoroughly mixed together.

4. Get a cookie sheet and line it with parchment paper. Proceed to grab a cookie scooper with which to apportion the dough onto the already lined cookie sheet.

5. Roll each scoop from the cookie scooper into a ball. Stick a toothpick through each ball to help ascertain doneness when refrigerating.

6. Take the rolled up balls one at a time, and dip into a bowl holding the melted chocolate. Return the chocolate dipped balls to the cookie sheet.

7. Proceed to store the chocolate dipped balls in the refrigerator to cool and become firm.

8. Once firm, serve as desired. You can also store leftovers in an airtight container in your fridge for as long as 5 days.

Note:

Tuna Melt Sandwich

(Time: 25 minutes)

Nutritional value per serving

One serving contains:

- 37.2 grams of total fat

- 11.9 grams of protein

- 698.6 milligrams of sodium

- 36.9 grams of total carbohydrates — 7.9 grams of total sugars

- 92.5 milligrams of cholesterol

- 551 calories

Total servings: 4

Utensils to use are:

- Knife — To cut ingredients

- Oven — To bake the buns

- Sheet pan — To hold the buns

Ingredients to use are:

For the tuna mixture

- ½ cup of salad green or arugula

- ½ cup of mayonnaise

- 2 to 3 chopped pickles (small variety)

- ¼ tsp of salt (kosher variety)

- 4 chopped celery stalks

- ¼ tsp of pepper (black variety)

- 2 tbsp of chopped fresh parsley

- 2 cans of Wild Selections Solid White Albacore Tuna in Water (5 ounces)

- 1 tbsp of lemon juice

- 1 peeled and chopped hard boiled egg

For the sandwich

- 1 thinly sliced cucumber

- 1 tomato, cut into slices (large size)

- 4 cornichons (pickled cucumbers) to be used as a garnish, optional

- 8 slices of cheddar, havarti, provolone, or mozzarella cheese

- ½ cup of salad greens or arugula

- 4 hamburger buns, halved

- 1 avocado, sliced (ripened variety)

Directions for preparation

1. Slice a bun into two equal halves. Top the bottom half with 1 slice of cheese and ½ cup of the Wild Selections Solid White Albacore Tuna in Water.

2. Take the top part of the bun and place on it a slice of cheese. Proceed to place both top and bottom halves of the buns on a sheet pan. Carry out the same process for the remaining buns.

3. Bake the buns in the oven preheated to 350°F for about 8 to 10 minutes until the cheese melts. Remove the buns from the oven and let sit to cool.

4. Proceed to assemble the sandwich. Top all bottom half buns (the part containing the tuna mix) with slices of tomato, salad greens or arugula, avocado, and cucumber.

5. Replace the top half buns on the bottom half to close off the sandwich. Add a bit of garnish like cornichon if you wish, and serve.

Note:

Basil Chicken Banh Mi Sandwich

(Time: 30 minutes)

Nutritional value per serving

One serving contains:

- 15.9 grams of total fat — 2.9 grams of saturated fat, 1.8 grams of monounsaturated fat, and 1.4 grams of polyunsaturated fat

- 64.1 grams of Protein 64.1 g

- 63.1 grams of Total Carbohydrate — 7.2 grams of dietary fibre, and 11.9 grams of total sugars

- 1130.9 milligrams of sodium

- 140.7 milligrams of Cholesterol

- 397 calories

Total servings: 4

Utensils to use are:

- Bowl (small and medium size) — To hold and mix the ingredients

- Skillet — To cook the ingredients

- Fork — To whisk ingredients

Ingredients to use are:

- Salt (kosher variety)

- 1 thinly sliced mango

- 2 tbsp of maple syrup

- 1 pinch of pepper (black variety)

- ¼ cup of tahini

- 2 tablespoons of chili garlic sauce

- 1 tbsp of toasted sesame seeds

- 2 tsp of garlic chili sauce (sambal oelek)

- 2 tablespoons of sesame oil

- ½ cup of fresh basil and cilantro leaves

- ¼ cup of chopped fresh basil

- 2 tablespoons of fish or soy sauce

- 1 thinly sliced jalapeño

- 1 lime, juiced

- 4 fried eggs, for serving (optional)

- 2 grated or minced cloves of garlic

- 2 tsp of maple syrup

- 1 pound of chicken breasts, cut into strips (boneless skinless variety)

- 1 quartered baguette and toasted pickled vegetables, for serving

Directions for preparation

1. Get a bowl (small size) and pour in 2 tbsp of water. Add 2 tbsp of chili garlic sauce, 2 garlic cloves, minced or grated, 2 tbsp of maple syrup, and 2 tbsp of fish or soy sauce. Sprinkle with a pinch of pepper. Toss the bowl until evenly mixed.

2. Place a skillet over medium high heat and pour in 2 tbsp of sesame oil. Add the chicken when the oil begins to simmer, not smoke. Cook for about 5 minutes until brown, and season with black pepper.

3. Gently pour in the already mixed sauce. Allow to simmer and cook for another 3 to 5 minutes until the chicken is evenly coated with the sauce.

4. Turn off the heat and stir in ¼ cup of chopped fresh basil to mix evenly.

5. Get another bowl (medium sized) and add in 1 mango cut into thin slices, 1 jalapeño, thinly sliced, 1 tbsp of toasted sesame seeds, and ½ cup of basil and cilantro leaves. Drizzle with lime juice and sprinkle with a pinch of kosher salt to taste. Work mixture by tossing until it is completely mixed.

6. Proceed to make the special sauce by combining all the ingredients into a large bowl. Get a fork and pour in ¼ cup of water. Beat the mixture until the desired consistency is achieved. Add more water when necessary.

7. Taste the sauce and adjust the seasonings to your desired taste.

8. Get your toasted baguette and spread with the special sauce. Garnish with slices of mango, chicken strips, fried eggs, and pickled vegetables.

9. Replace the top half on the bottom half of the sandwich. Best consumed immediately. Refrigerate leftovers.

Note:

Salted Butterscotch and Pecan Cookies

(Time: 25 minutes)

Nutritional value per serving

One serving (1 cookie) contains:

- 6 grams of total fat — 2 grams of saturated fat

- 1 gram of protein

- 8 grams of total carbohydrate — 7 grams of total sugars, and 1 gram of dietary fibre

- 104 milligrams of sodium

- 3 milligrams of cholesterol

- 88 calories

Total servings: 4 dozen (48 cookies)

Utensils to use are:

- Food processor — To blitz the ingredients

- Bowl (large size) — To hold the ingredients

- Baking pan — To hold the nuts

- Oven — To toast the nuts

- Skillet — To cook nuts

Ingredients to use:

- ½ cup of sugar

- 48 toasted pecan halves

- 1½ cups of finely shredded coconut (unsweetened variety)

- 1¾ cups of toasted pecans

- 1 packet of instant butterscotch pudding mix (3.4 ounces)

- 1½ teaspoons of salt (kosher variety)

- 1 can of sweetened milk (14 ounces) (condensed variety)

Directions for preparation

1. Get a food processor and pour in 1¾ cups of pecans. Sprinkle with kosher salt, and blitz to obtain a finely ground pecans mix.

2. Move the ground pecans to a large bowl and pour in 1 can of sweetened condensed milk, 1 packet of instant butterscotch pudding mix, and 1½ cups of finely shredded coconut (unsweetened variety). Stir until well blended.

3. Refrigerate for some minutes until the mixture is firm enough to be rolled up.

4. Cut and shape the mixture into 48 1 inch balls. Roll the balls in sugar, and top off each one with a pecan half. Proceed to slightly flatten the balls.

5. Store leftovers in an airtight container and refrigerate for up to 5 days.

Recipe tips

- To toast the pecan halves, spread the nuts 15 by 10 1 inch baking pan. Proceed to bake the nuts for 5 to 10 minutes at a temperature of 350°F until the nuts begin brown slightly. Stir regularly.

- You can also toast with a dry skillet (non-stick variety). Place the skillet over low heat and proceed to heat the nuts. Stir regularly until the nuts begin to brown.

- To get coconut (unsweetened variety), check the health food or baking section of a supermarket.

Note:

German Vegetarian Tomato Spread

(Time: 30 minutes)

Nutritional value per serving

One serving contains:

- 2 grams of total fat

- 2 grams of protein

- 10 grams of total carbohydrates

- 56 calories

Total servings: 1 cup spread (8 servings)

Utensils to use are:

- Saucepan (medium sized) — For sautéing

- Spoon — To stir

Ingredients to use:

- 2 tablespoons of tomato paste

106

- ¼ cup of sundried tomatoes (in oil, chopped finely)

- 1 finely chopped garlic clove

- ¼ tsp of salt (optional)

- 2 tablespoons of chopped fresh basil

- ¼ cup of chopped onion

- 2 tablespoons of whipping cream (30 to 36% milk fat)

- 2 teaspoons of good quality olive oil

- Freshly ground pepper to taste

- 1 can of tomatoes (14-ounce), or home-canned tomatoes, drained, but reserved with juices, and chopped, or 3 to 4 fresh tomatoes

Directions for preparation

1. Get a saucepan (medium sized) and place over a cooker. Pour in 2 teaspoons of good-quality olive oil and sauté 1 finely chopped garlic clove and ¼ cup of chopped onions until they become translucent.

2. Dice 4 seeded, blanched, or fresh tomatoes and drain to reserve their liquid. Add the drained,

diced tomatoes to the sautéing mixture in the saucepan.

3. Add ¼ cup of 2 tablespoons of tomato paste, and finely chopped sundried tomatoes, and cook by adding the reserved liquid from the diced tomatoes until the vegetables become tender.

4. Continue to cook until excess liquid is cooked off and a thick paste is formed. Proceed to add 2 tablespoons of whipping cream. Stir with a spoon until evenly mixed.

5. Turn down the heat and allow to sit and cool. Taste and adjust the seasonings to your desired preference.

6. Add 2 tablespoons of chopped fresh basil and stir. Store in a refrigerator and serve cold.

7. Consume within 3 days or freeze in ice-cube trays in tbsp as sandwich fillings.

Recipe tips:

- If you prefer your spread to be smoother, consider finely chopping all your veggies beforehand.

- For an even smoother spread, you can use an immersion blender or a food processor to blitz your veggies.

Serving Ideas With German Vegetarian Tomato Spread:

- Protein dipping: Use the tomato spread as dip for slices of hard boiled eggs.

- Simple tomato spread sandwich: Use the tomato spread alone between slices of bread.

- Fancy Sandwich: Use as a spread for sandwich. Cut buns in half and coat the cut surface of each half with tomato spread. Proceed to add slices of bell pepper and mozzarella (or any cheese of your choice), zucchini, and grilled eggplant

- Hot sauce: Coat a piece of bread with the tomato spread, and top off with any grated cheese of your choosing. Proceed to broil the bread for a couple of minutes.

Note:

Five Layer Mexican Dip

(Time: 23 minutes)

Nutritional value per serving

One serving contains:

- 5 grams of protein

- 15 grams of carbohydrates - 5 grams of fiber

- 6 milligrams of cholesterol

- 8 grams of fat - 2 grams of saturated fat

- 245 milligrams of sodium

- 140 calories

Total servings: 12

Utensils to use are:

- 1 chopping board

- 1 medium sized kitchen knife

- 1 skillet

- Food processor

- 1 small and 1 medium bowl

- 8 x 8 serving dish

Ingredients to use are:

- ¾ cup of shredded sharp cheese

- 2 tsp of olive oil

- 1 tbsp of diced jalapeno pepper

- 1 chopped medium onions

- ¼ cup of finely chopped scallion

- 2 chopped cloves of garlic

- 4 seeded and diced medium tomatoes

- 15.5 oz of black beans

- 2 ripe avocados

- 4 tbsp of lime juice

- ¼ cup of chopped cilantro

- 1 tbsp of diced chipotle pepper

- ¼ tsp of ground cumin

- 1 tbsp of water

- 2 cups of corn kernels

- ½ tsp of salt

Directions for preparation

1. Place your skillet on a stove set to medium-high heat and put some oil inside it. When it gets hot, add some onions inside the pan and sauté for 3 minutes. Next, add garlic and cook for 2 minutes more.

2. Turn your food processor on and put in ½ of the garlic mixture, black beans, chipotle pepper, 2 tbsp of lime juice, and cumin. Whisk until mixture is smooth.

3. Put your corn in the skillet alongside what remains of your garlic mixture and let it cook for 3 minutes. Then, turn the heat off before putting your cilantro leaves in and stirring.

4. Get your small bowl and put your avocado inside it. Also, add some lime juice. Mash the avocado. Put your jalapenos, tomatoes, and scallions in the medium bowl. You may want to add some salt and pepper. Mix well.

5. Spread the black beans mixture that is in your food processor in your serving dish. Spread the

corn mixture in your skillet over the black beans. Do the same with the avocado in your small bowl and jalapeno mixture in your medium bowl. Layer one evenly over the other. Sprinkle some grated cheese on top of it and serve. This goes well with some baked chips.

Note:

Polenta Squares with Mushroom Ragu

(Time: 30 minutes)

Nutritional value per serving

One serving contains:

- 1 gram of protein

- 2 grams of carbohydrates

- 1.5 grams of fat - 1 gram of saturated fat

- 0 grams of sugar

- 3 milligrams of cholesterol

- 86 milligrams of sodium

- 25 calories

Total servings: 36

Utensils to use are:

- 1 medium sized kitchen knife
- 1 chopping board
- 1 medium saucepan
- 1 whisk
- 1 large frying pan
- 9 x 9 inch baking pan

Ingredients to use are:

- 2 tbsp of diced fresh Italian parsley leaves
- 2 cups of water
- ½ tsp of all purpose flour
- 3 tbsp of butter
- ¾ cup of dry marsala
- ½ cup of polenta
- 1 diced clove of garlic
- 1 tbsp of olive oil
- ½ cup of chopped onion
- 8 oz of diced cremini mushrooms

- Sine salt and pepper

Directions for preparation

1. In the saucepan, add a cup of water, 1 tbsp of butter, and ½ tsp of salt. Mix and allow to boil. When the water starts to boil, reduce the heat to medium, add polenta and slowly whisk. You may have to stir for about 5 minutes before the polenta will get thick. Once that is done, pour into your baking pan and spread it well. Cove the pan and set it aside for the polenta to set.

2. Set your stove to medium-high heat and put a frying pan on it. Add some oil and, when it gets hot, put in your onions, mushrooms, and salt and pepper. Sauté for 8 minutes. Also, add garlic and sauté for 2 extra minutes. Put in your marsala and reduce the heat of the stove to medium. Cover the pan and allow to simmer for 5 minutes. In a small bowl, combine the all purpose flour and 2 tbsp of butter. Whisk well to make pasta. Stir as you turn this mixture into your simmering pan. Cover for 2 more minutes. By this time, the contents of the pan would have thickened. Turn off the heat and add parsley. Stir and add some pepper and salt. This is your ragu.

3. Once your polenta is set, it should be able to make 36 little squares. With a spoon, add some ragu on top of each polenta and serve.

Note:

Chapter 3:

Healthy Pasta

Recipes

Thank you for choosing this recipe book,
I hope it is useful for you.

,

I would like
have your own opinion on the recipes
you are going to prepare.
Your help will help me to improve
and deepen the arguments.

I thank you in advance if you want to help me
and enjoy your work.

Chicken and Broccoli Alfredo

(Time: 20 minutes)

Nutritional value per serving

One serving contains:

- 50 grams of carbohydrates - 4 grams of fiber

- 43 grams of protein

- 57 grams of fat

- 4 grams of sugar

- 854 calories

Total servings: 4

Utensils to use are:

- 1 chopping board

- 1 medium kitchen knife

- 1 large pot

- 1 colander

- 1 grater

Ingredients to use are:

- 0.5 pounds of spaghetti

- Some red pepper flakes

- 1 cup of broccoli florets (should fill two cups)

- 2 cups of Parmesan cheese, grated

- 2 tbsp of olive oil

- A quarter tsp of black pepper

- 2 chicken breasts, without their skin or bones. Add pepper to your desired taste

- A pinch of nutmeg

- ¼ cup of butter

- 3 diced cloves of garlic

- 1 cup of heavy cream

- Salt to desired taste

Directions for preparation

1. Set your stove to high heat. Pour some water into your pot, place it on the stove, and add some salt.

2. Now, parboil your spaghetti. This means you should cook it for about 6-7 minutes. Turn it down before it's soft and done.

3. Add broccoli to the spaghetti while it is still on the fire. Turn down the heat to medium-high and, after 4 minutes, take the pot off the stove.

4. Turn the contents of the pot into a colander and pour cold water into it.

5. Add some olive oil into your pot. When it's a little hot, put your chicken into the pot also. Add salt and pepper.

6. When your chicken is done, take it out of the pot and set aside.

7. Melt some butter into the pot, then add your diced garlic and fry for about 12 seconds. Continuously stir the garlic while frying.

8. Keep stirring as you put some nutmeg, heavy cream, pepper, and salt into the pot.

9. Once you notice this mixture bubbling, it's time to add your grated cheese. Stir until the contents of the pot become thick.

10. Add your spaghetti, broccoli, and chicken into the pot and make sure to mix them well together.

11. You may top this with some red pepper flakes and what is left of your Parmesan cheese.

Note:

Garlic Lemon Shrimp with Pasta

(Time: 30 minutes)

Nutritional value per serving

One serving contains:

- 54 grams of protein

- 43 grams of carbohydrates - 3 grams of fiber

- 20 grams of fat - 4 grams of saturated fat

- 349 milligrams of cholesterol

- 1147 milligrams of sodium

- 547 calories

Total servings: 4

Utensils to use are:

- A small grater

- A juicer

- 1 chopping board

- 1 medium kitchen knife

- 1 skillet

- 1 colander

Ingredients to use are:

- 12oz of spaghetti (the thin variety)

- ½ cup of shredded parmesan cheese

- 3 tbsp of olive oil

- One lemon, juiced

- 1 pound of peeled and deveined shrimp

- ¼ cup of white wine

- 2 finely chopped cloves of garlic

- 2 tbsp of fresh lemon zest

- ¼ tsp of red pepper flakes

- Ground black pepper and salt to desired taste

Directions for preparation

1. Set your stove to medium-high heat and cook your pasta according to the directions provided on the package. Take the pasta down before the center becomes soft.

2. Put some oil into a skillet at the same time you added pasta into boiling water. Sprinkle some pepper and salt on your shrimp and fry it in oil.

3. After about a minute and a half, flip the shrimp and continue frying. Add some more oil to this side of the shrimp. Also add your red pepper flakes, garlic, lemon zest, and white wine. Stir continuously for 30 seconds before adding lemon juice.

4. Now drain your pasta with a colander and place it in a bowl.

5. Add the shrimp sauce to the pasta and thoroughly toss it.

6. Pour a small quantity of olive oil on the meal before serving.

Note:

Vegan Creamy Mushroom Pasta

(Time: 25 minutes)

Nutritional value per serving

One serving contains:

- 17 grams of protein

- 104 grams of carbohydrates - 9 grams of fiber

- 20 grams of fat - 4 grams of saturated fat

- 9 milligrams of cholesterol

- 1822 milligrams of sodium

- 659 calories

Total servings: 4

Utensils to use are:

- 1 kitchen knife

- 1 chopping board

- 1 large ceramic pot

- 1 large saute pan

- 1 large bowl

- 1 balloon whisk

- 1 colander

Ingredients to use are;

- 16 oz of long thin pasta

- ¼ cup of sour cream, the non-dairy kind

- ¼ cup of soy margarine, the non-dairy kind

- 1 cup of soy milk

- 2 large finely chopped cloves of garlic

- 1 tbsp of all-purpose flour

- 16 oz of crimini mushrooms

- Kosher salt and ground black pepper to taste

Directions for preparation

1. Cook your pasta over medium heat and according to the directions on the package. Take the pot off the fire about 2 minutes before the time on the package directions. This is to ensure the pasta is al dente. That it, the pasta is only cooked

to the point where the outer layer is soft but the core is still, somewhat, resistant.

2. Drain the pasta in a colander.

3. Place your pan over medium-high heat and melt your soy margarine into it. Add your mushrooms and cloves of garlic into the pan and let it cook for about 5 minutes. Be careful to take out your mushrooms and garlic before they are overcooked. Your garlic should not be browned. Place them in a bowl once they are done.

4. Put some more margarine (about 2 tbsp) and flour into the saute pan over medium-high heat, and whisk for about a minute.

5. Add soy milk, salt, pepper, and sour cream to the flour mixture in the pan and stir well until it is smooth. Also, add mushrooms and garlic to the sauce and let it cook for about 3 minutes.

6. Now, add the pasta to the sauce and toss well. When serving, you can add some ground pepper to the pasta.

Note:

Tuna Carbonara

(Time: 30 minutes)

Nutritional value per serving

One serving contains:

- 36 grams of protein

- 52 grams of carbohydrates - 4 grams of fiber

- 29 grams of fat - 13 grams of saturated fat

- 646 milligrams of sodium

- 278 milligrams of cholesterol

- 621 calories

Total serving: 4

Utensils to use are:

- 1 small bowl

- A chopping board

- 1 small kitchen knife

- 1 grater

- 1 colander

- 1 large pot

- 1 saucepan

- I balloon whisk

Ingredients to use are:

- 1 chopped parsley (¼ cup)

- 43.3 oz spaghetti

- 1 cup of shredded parmesan cheese

- 4 slices of bacon

- 4 large eggs, beaten

- 1 can of white tuna

- 3 tbsp of heavy cream

- 1 diced onion

- 2 tbsp of melted butter

- 1 tbsp of olive oil

- 3 diced cloves of garlic

- 1 stripped red bell pepper

1. Set your stove to medium-high heat and put some salted water into it a large pot. Put your spaghetti in the water and, using the package cooking instructions as a guide, cook to al dente. Make sure your water exceeds the amount of pasta in the pot.

2. Drain the spaghetti and set half of cup of pasta water aside.

3. Put bacon slices into your saucepan and cook until they are crispy.

4. Set the bacon on some paper towels and leave it for a bit.

5. Drain all the fat from the saucepan, but leave about a tbsp.

6. Melt some butter and olive oil in your saucepan and fry your onion, bell pepper, and garlic in the pan.

7. Add your pasta into the saucepan. Also, add some tuna and toss to mix it all.

8. Thoroughly whisk your eggs and heavy cream in a bowl and add to the pasta in the saucepan. Make sure to coat the pasta well in the egg.

9. Add your cup of pasta water, bacon, cheese, and parsley. Cook and toss until the cheese melts.

Note:

Penne all'Arrabbiata

(Time: 20 minutes)

Nutritional value per serving

One serving contains:

- 19 grams of protein

- 16 grams of fat - 5 grams of saturated fat

- 71 grams of carbohydrates - 5 grams of fiber

- 391 milligrams of sodium

- 15 milligrams of cholesterol

- 496 calories

Total servings: 6

Utensils to use are:

- 1 chopping board

- 1 medium kitchen knife

- 1 large pot

- 1 saucepan

- 1 colander

Ingredients to use are:

- 1 cup of sheep's milk cheese and cow's milk dry cheese, mixed

- 16 oz of penne pasta

- 6 chopped, fresh basil leaves

- ¼ cup of olive oil

- 11 oz of seeded, peeled, and chopped tomatoes

- 2 diced cloves of garlic

- 2 minced hot chile peppers to taste

- Salt to taste

Directions for preparation

1. Place a pot of salted water over medium-high heat to boil.

2. Cook your pasta to al dente and drain it with a colander.

3. Place a saucepan containing about 2 tbsp of oil on a stove set to medium heat and saute your

garlic and onions in it. It should take about 2 minutes for them to turn slightly brown.

4. Add your minced chile peppers and continue frying for about 40 seconds.

5. Now, reduce the heat of the stove to low and add your tomatoes.

6. Add some basil and what is left of your oil into the saucepan.

7. Pour your pasta into the sauce and mix them well.

8. When serving, you may like to sprinkle some shredded cheese on the pasta. Some white wine would go well with this dish.

Note:

Ravioli with Sun-dried Tomatoes, Arugula and Hazelnuts

(Time: 15 minutes)

Nutritional value per serving

One serving contains:

- 11 grams of protein
- 31 grams of carbohydrates - 5 grams of fiber
- 36 grams of fat - 5 grams of saturated fat
- 23 milligrams of cholesterol
- 455 milligrams of sodium
- 8 grams of sugar
- 470 calories

Total servings: 4

Utensils to use are:

- A chopping board

- 1 medium kitchen knife

- 1 large pot

- 1 large serving bowl

- 1 colander

Ingredients to use are:

- 16 oz of mozzarella ravioli

- 6 tbsp of olive oil

- 1 cup of sun-dried tomatoes, thin slices

- 1 cup of arugula leaves

- Half a cup of hazelnuts, chopped and toasted

- Ground black pepper and kosher salt to taste

Directions for preparation

1. Set your stove to medium-high heat, place a pot of salted water on it, and cook your ravioli in accordance with the instructions on the package. Just take care to not let the ravioli get too soft. Drain the ravioli.

2. In your large bowl, put in your sun-dried tomatoes, arugula leaves, chopped hazelnuts, and salt and pepper. Mix them well. Add some olive oil and continue gently stirring.

3. Add the ravioli to the arugula mixture in the bowl and toss.

4. You may choose to add some shredded parmesan cheese to this meal.

Note:

_____

_____

_____

_____

_____

_____

Hummus Linguini with Zucchini

(Time: 25 minutes)

Nutritional value per serving

One serving contains:

- 10 grams of protein
- 40 grams of carbohydrates - 2 grams of fiber
- 4 grams of fat - 1 gram of saturated fat
- 4 milligrams of cholesterol
- 283 milligrams of sodium
- 2 grams of sugar
- 224 calories

Total servings: 8

Utensils to use are:

- 1 medium pot
- 1 colander
- 1 large skillet, the nonstick kind

Ingredients to use are:

- ¼ cup of chopped leaf parsley

- 13.0 oz of whole wheat linguine

- Half an onion, finely chopped

- 2 tsp of olive oil

- ¼ cup of crumbled feta cheese

- 2 diced cloves of garlic

- 2 tbsp of rice vinegar

- ¼ tsp of red pepper flakes

- ½ cup of hummus

- 4 cups of zucchini which has been julienned

- 1 cup of vegetable broth

- Salt and pepper to desired taste

Directions for preparation

1. Set your stove to medium-high heat and cook your linguine according the the directions written on the package.

2. Place your skillet over medium-high heat and add some extra virgin olive oil to it.

3. Add red pepper flakes, onions, and garlic to the hot oil and stir for 2 minutes.

4. Add hummus, zucchinis, rice vinegar, and vegetable broth into the skillet and cook for 4 minutes.

5. Put your feta cheese and parsley inside the sauce. Also, add your linguine. Add some salt and pepper to your taste.

6. Toss the pasta until it mixes well with the sauce. Let it cook for a minute and a half before turning off the heat.

Note:

Sweet Potato Noodles

(Time: 25 minutes)

Nutritional value per serving

One serving contains:

- 35.9 grams of carbohydrates - 1 gram of fiber

- 2 grams of fat - 0.2 grams of saturated fat

- 7.4 grams of protein

- 3.9 grams of sugar

- 675.5 milligrams of sodium

- 13.5 milligrams of cholesterol

- 189.2 calories

Total serving: 6

Utensils to use are:

- A chopping board

- 1 medium kitchen knife

- 1 large sized ceramic pot

- 1 medium sized bowl

- 1 large skillet of the nonstick variety

- 1 colander

- Tongs

Ingredients to use are:

- 0.5 pounds of sweet potato noodles

- 1 cup of fresh spinach

- 2 half tsp of sesame oil

- 2 peeled and thin sliced medium carrots

- ¼ cup of soy sauce

- Half red bell pepper, diced

- 2 tsp of honey

- 1 chicken breast without bones or skin

- 1 tsp of canola oil

- 2 diced cloves of garlic

Directions for preparation

1. Put the pot on the stove set to medium-high heat. Boil your potato noodles in the pot for a total of 5 minutes before draining it. Rinse your noodles with cold water from the tap, add half a tsp of canola oil and toss.

2. Put your soy sauce and honey in a bowl and mix them.

3. Put the remaining half of your canola oil in a skillet. When it's hot enough (about 30 seconds after), put in your chicken and cook for 3 minutes. Make sure to flip to cook all the sides of the chicken.

4. Add spinach, red pepper, garlic, and carrots into the skillet and continue cooking.

5. Now, add your honey mixture and some sesame oil before throwing in your noodles and tossing to ensure they mix well together.

6. After 4 more minutes of cooking, turn off the heat.

Note:

Chinese Noodles with Bok Choy and Hoisin Sauce

(Time: 30 minutes)

Nutritional value per serving

One serving contains:

- 15 grams of protein
- 5 grams of fat - 1 gram of saturated fat
- 56 grams of carbohydrates - 2 grams of fiber
- 4 grams of sugar
- 21 milligrams of cholesterol
- 625 milligrams of sodium
- 184 milligrams of potassium
- 327 calories

Total servings: 7

Utensils to use are:

- 1 colander
- 1 medium kitchen knife

- I medium bowl

- 1 large pot

- tongs

- 1 large skillet

- 1 balloon whisk

Ingredients to use are:

- 1 pound of Chinese noodles

- ¼ cup of Hoisin sauce

- 3 tsp of canola oil

- 2 ½ tsp of soy sauce

- 1 tbsp of diced ginger

- 1 tbsp of rice vinegar

- 3 chopped cloves of garlic

- 2 tsp of rice wine

- 2 cut chicken breasts that are without bones or skin

- ½ tsp of sesame oil

- 1 pound of minced bok choy

- ¼ tsp of garlic sauce

- 10 diced spears of corn

Directions for preparation

1. Over medium-high heat, cook your Chinese noodles according to the directions on the package. When they are tender (not mushy), drain in a colander and rinse with cold water.

2. Put your rice vinegar, soy sauce, rice wine, Hoisin sauce, garlic sauce, and sesame oil in a bowl. Mix them well together and set aside.

3. Place your skillet over medium-high heat and put 2 tsp of oil in it. Cook your ginger and garlic in it for about 40 seconds.

4. Add the chicken into the skillet and cook for 4 minutes. Remember to flip the chicken. Take the chicken from the skillet and place it in a bowl.

5. With a colander, rinse your bok choy. Pour it into your skillet, along with your canola oil and corn. Stir for about a minute over medium heat.

6. Add your noodles, Hoisin sauce mixture, and chicken into the skillet.

7. With tongs, toss the noodles well.

8. Your meal is ready to be served.

Note:

Marmite Carbonara

(Time: 20 minutes)

Nutritional value per serving

One serving contains:

- 21.3 grams of protein

- 22.2 grams of fat - 6.2 grams of saturated fat

- 56.5 grams of carbohydrates - 3.3 grams of fiber

- 2.1 grams of sugar

- 518 calories

Total servings: 2

Utensils to use are:

- 1 grater

- 1 medium knife

- 1 chopping board

- 1 large pot

- 1 colander

- 1 medium sized bowl

- 1 large skillet

Ingredients to use are:

- yolks of 2 large eggs

- ¼ cup of diced parsley

- 2 tsp of Marmite

- 2 tbsp of olive oil

- 6 oz of spaghetti

- 1 oz of chopped parmesan

- 1 crushed clove of garlic

- Some ground pepper

Directions for preparation

1. After boiling your pasta until it's tender and according to the directions on the package, drain it. Set some pasta water (half a cup) aside.

2. Add the Marmite to your egg yolks that are in a bowl. Also add parmesan and pepper, and whisk.

3. Add 2 tbsp of oil to your pan and place it on a stove set to medium-high heat. When the oil is hot, put your clove of garlic into the pan and fry till it attains a light brown color. Once that is done, take out the garlic.

4. Turn off the heat and put the pasta into the pan. Also, add the egg mixture and some pasta water.

5. Toss the pasta well to ensure that no part of it is left uncoated.

6. You may sprinkle some shredded parmesan and parsley before serving.

Note:

Macadamia Pesto Pappardelle

(Time: 30 minutes)

Nutritional value per serving

One serving contains:

- 16.5 grams of protein

- 56.4 grams of carbohydrates - 4.9 grams of fiber

- 65.3 grams of fat - 11.7 grams of saturated fat

- 2.3 grams of sugar

- 889 calories

Total servings: 2

Utensils to use are:

- 1 medium kitchen knife

- 1 grater

- A juicer

- A food processor

- 1 medium sized bowl

- 1 medium sized pot

- 1 colander

Ingredients to use are:

- 5 oz of pappardelle

- 1 juiced lemon

- 0.8 oz of toasted macadamia nuts

- 1 oz of grated parmesan cheese

- 6 tbsp olive oil

- 1.5 oz of basil

- 1 crushed clove of garlic

- Salt to taste

Directions for preparation

1. Break up the nuts in a food processor.

2. Add garlic, basil, salt, and oil to the nuts and process the mixture some more.

3. Turn the contents of the food processor into a bowl, and add your parmesan cheese shavings and lemon juice.

4. Cook your pappardelle till it is tender and in accordance with the directions on the pack. Drain in a colander, but save some of the pasta water for later.

5. Turn your pappardelle into the bowl of basil mixture (pesto) and toss until the pasta is well coated. Add some of the pasta water while tossing, as it may be a little dry.

Note:

Macaroni and Cheese Topped with Salsa

(Time: 25 minutes)

Nutritional value per serving

One serving contains:

- 27.6 grams of protein

- 44.6 grams of carbohydrates - 3 grams of fiber

- 28.1 grams of fat - 16.6 grams of saturated fat

- 1.2 grams of sugar

- 547 calories

Total servings: 6

Utensils to use are:

- 1 grater

- 1 chopping board

- 1 medium sized kitchen knife

- 1 medium sized bowl

- 1 medium sized pot

Ingredients to use are:

- 1 small cup of red wine vinegar
- 3 cups of skimmed milk
- Olive oil
- 10.6 oz of macaroni
- 3.5 oz of soft cheese
- 7 oz of grated cheddar cheese
- 3.5 oz of grated emmental cheese
- 1. 8 oz of grated parmesan cheese
- 2 tbsp of diced coriander
- 3.5 oz of chopped cherry tomatoes
- Half an onion, chopped
- 3 tbsp of chopped, pickled jalapños

Directions for preparation

1. In a bowl, put in the tomatoes, coriander, jalapeños, onion, red wine vinegar, and oil. Mix well and set the salsa aside.

2. Over medium-high heat, place a pan containing milk and let it simmer for a bit. Put your macaroni in the pan and cook it in the milk. This should take about 10 minutes. Now add your soft cheese, and shredded cheddar, emmental, and parmesan cheeses. Stir them in the pan till they melt.

3. Add some pepper to your desired taste and serve with some of the earlier salsa placed on the macaroni.

Note:

Lemon Pepper Pasta with Shrimp

(Time: 15 minutes)

Nutritional value per serving

One serving contains:

- 37 grams of protein
- 44.8 grams of carbohydrates - 7.8 grams of fiber
- 16.8 grams of fat
- 2.3 grams of sugar
- 1233 milligrams of sodium
- 500 calories

Total servings: 3

Utensils to use are:

- 1 chopping board
- 1 medium kitchen knife
- 1 grater
- 1 medium pot

- 1 colander

- 1 large skillet, the nonstick kind

Ingredients to use are:

- ½ cup of parmesan cheese, shredded

- ½ pound of cavatappi

- ¼ cup of basil pesto

- Extra Virgin olive oil

- 1 pound of deveined and peeled shrimp

- Ground black pepper and salt to taste

- 1 lemon zest

- ⅓ cup of white wine

- 2 cups of spinach and kale, chopped

Directions for preparation

1. Allow a pot of salted water to boil over medium heat and cook your cavatappi according to the directions on the pack.

2. At the same time, put some oil in your skillet and when it is hot, add your shrimp and fry it for about 1 ½ minutes. Remember to flip the shrimp with a spoon while it is cooking.

3.Splash your wine into the pan. Also, add kale, lemon zest, ground black pepper and salt. Turn off the heat after 2 minutes.

4.Your shrimp should be tender by now. Drain and turn it inside the pan. Also, add basil pesto and your shredded cheese. Toss to ensure all is well incorporated.

Note:

Mushroom Spaghetti Aglio Olio

(Time: 15 minutes)

Nutritional value per serving

One serving contains:

- 10 grams of protein

- 49.8 grams of carbohydrates

- 2.7 grams of sugar

- 9.1 grams of fat

- 2.5 milligrams of cholesterol

- 598.9 milligrams of sodium

- 318 calories

Total servings: 4

Utensils to use are:

- 1 grater

- 1 medium sized pot

Ingredients to use are:

- 3 tbsp of grated parmesan cheese

- 9 oz of spaghetti

- 1 tsp of butter

- 7 oz of cut mushrooms

- 5 diced cloves of garlic

- Olive oil

- 1 ½ tsp of dried parsley

- ½ tsp of chilli flakes

- Salt to desired taste

Directions for preparation

1. In a pot of boiling, salted water, place your spaghetti and cook until it is tender on the outside but slightly tough at the core (al dente). Use the directions on the package as a guide.

2. Meanwhile, put some oil in a fry pan and place it over medium-high heat. Cook your mushrooms in the pan until all sides attain a slightly brown color.

3. Without placing them on top of the mushrooms, add your chilli, garlic, and what is left of your olive oil. Reduce the heat to medium-low and continue frying for about a minute. Now, add spaghetti and toss. Also, put in your parsley and butter. Add salt

to taste and mix the pasta with the other contents of the pan.

4. Once the pasta and herbs are well incorporated and the butter has melted, you can now turn off the heat and serve.

Note:

Creamy Salmon Orzo

(Time: 15 minutes)

Nutritional value per serving

One serving contains:

- 29.7 grams of protein

- 69.3 grams of carbohydrates - 7 grams of fiber

- 13.8 grams of sugar

- 18.1 grams of fat - 9 grams of saturated fat

- 41 milligrams of cholesterol

- 1059 milligrams of sodium

- 553 calories

Total servings: 4

Utensils to use are:

- 1 chopping board

- 1 medium sized kitchen knife

- 1 grater

- 1 medium deep skillet

- 1 whisk

Ingredients to use are:

- 1.41 oz of butter, unsalted kind

- 6 oz of smoked salmon

- ½ diced onion

- 2 diced cloves of garlic

- ½ cup is parmesan, shredded

- 1 tbsp of flour

- 2 cups of peas, frozen

- 2 cups of milk

- 1 ½ cups of dried orzo

- 2 ¼ cups of chicken broth

- Chopped parsley

Directions for preparation

1. Place your skillet over medium-high heat and place your unsalted butter in it. Let it melt, and fry your onions and garlic in it.

2. Put flour in the pan and, after a minute, add half the milk and whisk. About 30 seconds of whisking should be enough before you add chicken broth, orzo, peas, and the other half of your milk.

3. Reduce the heat to medium and let the contents of the pan simmer for 5 minutes. Stir from time to time during the 5 minute period.

4. Turn off the heat after that and take the pan off the heat.

5. Add parmesan cheese, salt, and pepper to the sauce and stir. Next, add your smoked salmon and stir.

6. You may sprinkle some parsley on the meal before serving.

Note:

Lemon Butter Garlic Shrimp with Pasta

(Time: 15 minutes)

Nutritional value per serving

One serving contains:

- 34 grams of protein

- 45 grams of carbohydrates - 2 grams of fiber

- 26 grams of fat - 15 grams of saturated fat

- 2 grams of sugar

- 1375 milligrams of sodium

- 552 calories

Total servings: 3

Utensils to use are:

- 1 medium pot

- 1 large skillet

- 1 colander

- 1 tong

Ingredients to use are:

- 8 oz of thin spaghetti (angel hair)
- ½ cup of unsalted butter
- Garlic powder to desired taste
- Lemon zest
- ¼ cup of lemon juice
- Pepper to desired taste
- Salt to desired taste
- 1 pound of peeled and deveined shrimp

Directions for preparation

1. Over medium-high heat, cook your spaghetti till it is tender. Follow the cooking instructions on the package. When it is done, drain the pasta and keep it aside for later.

2. Melt your unsalted butter in the pan and add garlic powder to the oil.

3. Add shrimp and cook for about 3 minutes. Meanwhile, add some salt and pepper to your taste. Flip the shrimp to cook all sides.

4. Now, add lemon zest and juice, and stir.

5. Turn your pasta into the skillet and reduce the heat to medium-low. Toss it well with tongs. You

may add some more spices, salt, and juice if the meal does not meet your desired taste.

Note:

Penne Rosa

(Time: 30 minutes)

Nutritional value per serving

One serving contains:

- 20 grams of protein

- 71 grams of carbohydrates - 4 grams of fiber

- 6 grams of sugar

- 12 grams of fat - 5 grams of saturated fat

- 575 milligrams of sodium

- 31 milligrams of cholesterol

- 477 calories

Total servings: 6

Utensils to use are:

- 1 grater

- 1 medium sized kitchen knife

- 1 chopping board

- 1 large skillet

- 1 medium sized pot

Ingredients to use are:

- ½ cup of grated parmesan

- 1 pound of penne pasta

- ½ cup of heavy cream

- Olive oil

- 3 cups of spinach leaves

- 8 oz of diced mushrooms

- 4 chopped roma tomatoes

- ½ tsp of crushed red pepper flakes

- 2 crushed cloves of garlic

- 1 ½ cups of marinara

Directions for preparation

1.Cook your pasta in accordance with the instructions on the pack till it's tender.

2. While the pasta is cooking, sauté your mushrooms in the skillet over medium-high heat. Do this till the mushrooms are tender.

3. Add your garlic into the pan and keep cooking for about a minute. Also, add marinara and pepper flakes. Put in your tomatoes, heavy cream, and spinach and stir.

4. Next, turn your pasta into the pan and toss well to ensure it is properly coated.

5. You can turn off the heat now. Sprinkle some cheese on the pasta and serve.

Note:

Chapter 4:

Healthy Salad

Recipes

Thank you for choosing this recipe book,
I hope it is useful for you.

,

I would like
have your own opinion on the recipes
you are going to prepare.
Your help will help me to improve
and deepen the arguments.

I thank you in advance if you want to help me
and enjoy your work.

Romaine Salad with Lemon-Pecorino Vinaigrette

(Time: 20 minutes)

Nutritional value per serving

One serving contains:

- 3 grams of protein

- 3 grams of carbohydrates - 1 grams of fiber

- 8.5 grams of fat - 1.5 grams of saturated fat

- 105 milligrams of sodium

- 95 calories

Total servings: 8

Utensils to use:

- 1 medium sized kitchen knife

- 1 grater

- 1 chopping board

- 1 small bowl

- 1 large bowl

Ingredients to use are:

- ¼ toasted and chopped hazelnuts

- 1 thin sliced red onions

- 8 cups romaine lettuce hearts

- 4 tbsp of sherry vinegar

- ½ cups of grated pecorino cheese

- 3 tbsp of Extra Virgin olive oil

- 1 tsp Dijon mustard

- 1 crushed cloves garlic

Directions for preparation

1. Put some onion, vinegar, and salt into a bowl and mix well. Then, set the bowl aside.

2. Get a larger bowl and put some oil, mustard, vinegar, garlic, and pecorino inside it.

3. Drain your onions from the smaller bowl and sprinkle them over the contents of the large bowl. Also, add lettuce, hazelnuts, and more pecorino to the salad.

Note:

Healthy Coleslaw

(Time: 10 minutes)

Nutritional value per serving

One serving contains:

- 1.7 grams of protein

- 5.8 grams of carbohydrates

- 3.5 grams of sugar

- 1 grams of fat

- 4 milligrams of cholesterol

- 41 calories

Total servings: 6

Utensils to use are:

- 1 small bowl

- 1 whisk

- 1 large bowl

Ingredients to use are:

- 6 cups of coleslaw

- 1 tbsp of honey

- ¾ cup of whole plain yogurt

- 2 tsp of vinegar

- 2 tsp of lemon juice

- Ground black pepper and salt to taste

Directions for preparation

1. Put your honey, whole plain yogurt, vinegar, and lemon juice in a bowl. Also, add salt and pepper, and whisk this mixture. This is your coleslaw dressing.

2. Get a large bowl and put your coleslaw in the bowl. Add the dressing and toss. Leave it for about 5 minutes before tossing it again.

3. You may choose to keep the dressing in your refrigerator for as many as 3 days until you are ready to toss your coleslaw into it and serve.

Note:

Black Bean Mango Salad

(Time: 15 minutes)

Nutritional value per serving

One serving contains:

- 7.6 grams of protein

- 38.8 grams of carbohydrates

- 19 grams of sugar

- 5.8 grams of fat

- 323.3 milligrams of sodium

- 222 calories

Total servings: 6

Utensils to use are:

- 1 chopping board

- 1 medium sized kitchen knife

- 1 large bowl

Ingredients to use are:

- 2 tsp of ground cumin

- 2 medium chopped mangoes

- 1 juiced lime

- 1 chopped large tomato

- 1 chopped large bell pepper

- 1 cup of cooked corn

- 2 tbsp of olive oil

- 19 oz of rinsed black beans

- 2 tbsp of diced onions

- ½ cup of diced cilantro

- Salt and hot pepper chilli flakes to taste

Directions for preparation

1. Put tomato, bell pepper, cilantro, onions, black beans, olive oil, lime juice, cumin, corn, mango, salt, and pepper in a large bowl. Toss gently and your salad is ready to be served.

Note:

Charred Shrimp and Avocado Salad

(Time: 25 minutes)

Nutritional value per serving

One serving contains:

- 35 grams of protein
- 20 grams of carbohydrates - 4 grams of fiber
- 23.5 grams of fat - 3.5 grams of saturated fat
- 1595 milligrams of sodium
- 420 calories

Total servings: 4

Utensils to use are:

- 1 chopping board
- 1 medium sized kitchen knife
- 1 grill pan
- 1 large bowl
- 1 whisk

Ingredients to use are:

- 1 avocado, cut into four parts
- 2 ½ pounds of deveined and peeled shrimp
- ½ bunch of Upland watercress
- 5 tbsp of olive oil
- ½ sliced English cucumber
- ½ finely chopped red onions
- 2 tbsp of lemon juice
- ½ peeled and sliced pineapple
- Salt and pepper to preferred taste

Directions for preparation

1. Coat your shrimp in 2 tbsp of oil and add salt and pepper as you desire. Also coat your pineapple in oil and place both the shrimp and pineapple in your grill pan. Now, grill for about 8 minutes. Make sure you rotate the pan to cook all the sides of the food. Your pineapple should end up a little charred.

2. Get a large bowl and put in the lemon juice, salt, pepper, onions, and oil. Toss this mixture well.

3. Cut your charred pineapple into little pieces and put them in the bowl. Also, add cucumber,

watercress, shrimp, and avocado and toss this well together.

Note:

Mixed Green and Herb Toss Salad

(Time: 10 minutes)

Nutritional value per serving

One serving contains:

- 3 grams of protein

- 10 grams of fat - 1 gram of saturated fat

- 6 grams of carbohydrates - 2 grams of fiber

- 180 milligrams of sodium

- 125 calories

Total servings: 6

Utensils to use are:

- 1 chopping board

- 1 juicer

- 2 large bowl

- 1 medium sized kitchen knife

- 1 whisk

Ingredients to use are:

- Soft boiled eggs

- 6 cups of Bibbs and mâche, mixed

- 1 small, chopped shallot

- 2 cups of chopped tarragon, chives, and mint, mixed

- 1 tsp of honey

- 1 cup of edamame, shelled

- 2 tsp of Dijon mustard

- ¼ cup of olive oil

- 1 tbsp of lemon juice

- Kosher salt and pepper to preferred taste

Directions for preparation

1. In a large bowl, put in your mâche, Bibb, tarragon, chives, mint, and edamame. Mix them up.

2. In a different bowl, put in your olive oil, mustard, lemon juice, salt, honey, pepper, and shallots. Stir to mix well. This is the salad dressing.

3. Place the dressing on the salad and stir some more. Cut your boiled eggs in halves and place on the salad.

Note:

Chicken and Red Plum Salads

(Time: 20 minutes)

Nutritional value per serving

One serving contains:

- 38 grams of protein

- 12 grams of carbohydrates - 3 grams of fiber

- 16.5 grams of fat - 2.5 grams of saturated fat

- 345 milligrams of sodium

- 355 calories

Total servings: 4

Utensils to use are:

- 1 chopping board

- 1 medium sized kitchen knife

- 1 large bowl

Ingredients to use are:

- ¼ cups of chopped, roasted almonds

- 6 oz of chicken breasts, without skin or bones

- ½ cup of chopped fresh dill

- 2 tbsp of Extra Virgin olive oil

- 6 cups of baby arugula

- 4 cut red plums

- Salt and pepper to taste

- 2 finely diced scallions

Directions for preparation

1. Coat your chicken with a tsp of oil and add a pinch of salt and pepper to the chicken (or add to your desired taste).

2. Get a large bowl and put your plums, ½ tsp of oil, salt, and pepper inside. Toss well.

3. Grill your chicken for about 10 minutes. Make sure both sides are cooked. Next, take the chicken and place it on your chopping board. After setting it aside for about 5 minutes, slice it.

4. Now grill your red plums for 4 minutes. After that, put them back inside your bowl and add what is left of your oil and the scallions to it. Mix well.

5. Add chicken, arugula, almonds, and dill to the bowl and toss well.

Note:

Chapter 5:

Healthy Meat

Recipes

Thank you for choosing this recipe book,

I hope it is useful for you.

,

I would like

have your own opinion on the recipes

you are going to prepare.

Your help will help me to improve

and deepen the arguments.

I thank you in advance if you want to help me
and enjoy your work.

Cheesy Meatball Skillet

(Time: 30 minutes)

Nutritional value per serving

One serving contains:

- 57.9 grams of protein

- 36.7 grams of carbohydrates - 5.1 grams of fiber

- 16.7 grams of sugar

- 24.5 grams of fat - 11.4 grams of saturated fat

- 181 milligrams of cholesterol

- 1361 milligrams of sodium

- 606 calories

Total servings: 4

Utensils to use are:

- 1 grater

- 1 chopping board

- 1 medium sized kitchen knife

- Paper towels

- 1 large bowl

- 1 ice cream scoop

- 1 large skillet

Ingredients to use are:

- 24 oz of marinara sauce

- ½ cup of shredded parmesan cheese

- 1 cup of grated mozzarella cheese

- ½ cup of Italian bread crumbs

- 1 tbsp of chopped fresh basit

- 1 tbsp of Worcestershire sauce

- 1 pound of ground beef

- 1 beaten large egg

- 1 tbsp of diced garlic

Directions for preparation

1. In the large bowl, put your beef, garlic, bread crumbs, parmesan cheese, egg, Worcestershire sauce, salt, and pepper. Mix them well.

2. Take an ice cream scoop-full of the mixture and roll it with your hands to form meatball shapes.

3. Place your skillet over medium-high heat and pour some oil inside it. Next, put your meatballs in

the skillet and fry until they are brown. This could take up to 8 minutes.

4. Put the meatballs on your paper towels to drain. After taking out the oil from the pan, add marinara sauce and reduce the stove to medium-low heat.

5. Take your meatballs from the paper towels and place them, batch by batch, in the pan. Make sure each one of them is evenly coated in the sauce. Let each batch simmer for 8 minutes.

6. Also, top each batch of meatballs with mozzarella cheese and let it simmer until the mozzarella melts into the meatballs.

7. Sprinkle some basil on the meatballs when serving.

Note:

Swedish Meatballs

(Time: 30 minutes)

Nutritional value per serving

One serving contains:

- 32.6 grams of protein

- 25.7 grams of carbohydrates - 1.3 grams of fiber

- 2.8 grams of sugar

- 28.4 grams of fat - 14.9 grams of saturated fat

- 189.6 milligrams of cholesterol

- 663.2 milligrams of sodium

- 553.8 calories

Total servings: 6

Utensils to use are:

- 1 chopping board

- 1 kitchen knife

- 1 large skillet, non-stick kind

- 1 wooden spoon

- 1 large bowl

- Ice cream scoop

- 1 balloon whisk

Ingredients to use are:

- 2 tbsp of chopped parsley leaves

- 2 tbsp of olive oil

- 4 cups of beef broth

- 1 diced onions

- ⅓ cups of all purpose flour

- 1 pound of ground beef

- ¼ cup of unsalted butter

- ½ cup of panko

- ¼ tsp of ground allspice

- Some salt and pepper to taste

- 2 large egg yolks

- ¼ tsp of ground nutmeg

- ¾ cups of sour cream

Directions for use

1. Place a skillet over medium-high heat and pour a tbsp of oil in it. Put some onions inside the pan and saute for 3 minutes.

2. Now, put ground beef, yolks, breadcrumbs, ground pork, allspice, cooked onions, salt, pepper, and nutmeg inside a bowl. Stir with a wooden spoon and use an ice cream scoop to form about 24 meatballs.

3. Put some oil into the skillet and place your meatballs in it. Brown for 4 minutes before placing them in a place lined with paper towels.

4. For the preparation of your gravy, put some butter in a skillet and melt it. Also, add flour and whisk for a minute until it turns a light brown. Add your beef broth and continue to whisk for 2 minutes. Add sour cream and your preferred quantity of salt and pepper.

5. Put your meatballs in the gravy and continue cooking and stirring for 8 minutes. By that time, the meatballs should have thickened.

6. Sprinkle some parsley and serve.

Note:

Meatballs In Creamy Dill Sauce

(Time: 24 minutes)

Nutritional value per serving

One serving contains:

- 12 grams of total fat — 5 grams of saturated fat

- 45 grams of total carbohydrates — 3 grams of dietary fibre

- 37 grams of protein

- 798 milligrams of sodium

- 181 milligrams of cholesterol

- 448 calories

Total servings: 4

Utensils to use are:

- Bowl (large sized) — To mix the ingredients

- Skillet (large sized, monsters variety) — To cook the ingredients

- Thermometer — To measure temperature

Ingredients to use are:

- 1 pound of lean ground beef

- ⅓ cup of bread crumbs

- ¼ cup of milk (fat-free variety)

- 2 tablespoons of snipped fresh dill

- Mushrooms, sliced and drained (4 ounces)

- ½ teaspoon of black pepper

- 1 medium onion, sliced thinly

- 1 egg

- 2 cups of beef broth (reduced-sodium variety)

- 2 tablespoons of flour (all-purpose variety)

- ¼ cup of sour cream (reduced-fat variety)

- ½ teaspoon of salt

- Egg noodles, cooked according to the directions on the packet (6 ounces)

- Steamed broccoli (optional)

Directions for preparation

1. Get a bowl (large sized) and break the egg into it. Sprinkle with bread crumbs and add milk, beef, ¼ tsp of pepper and salt to taste. Mix well and roll into meatballs (about 16).

2. Get a skillet (large sized, nonstick variety) and place over medium high heat. Coat the skillet with cooking spray.

3. Add in the onions and cook for about 2 minutes. Pour the broth into the flour and mix well.

4. Proceed to pour the broth and flour mixture into the skillet and leave to simmer.

5. Add the meatballs and mushrooms. Sprinkle with the remaining ¼ tsp of pepper and salt.

6. Cook for 12 minutes while ensuring you turn the meatballs regularly. Measure the temperature with a thermometer. When it reaches 160° F, proceed to add the sour cream. Turn down the heat and stir well to mix.

7. Serve with any noodles of your choice, or steamed broccoli.

Note:

Turkey Meatballs

(Time: 30 minutes)

Nutritional values per serving

One serving contains:

- 20 4 grams of protein
- 0.3 grams of carbohydrates - 0.1 grams of fiber
- 9.5 grams of fat - 2.5 grams of saturated fat
- 115.8 milligrams of cholesterol
- 343.8 milligrams of sodium
- 168 calories

Total servings: 47 meatballs

Utensils to use are:

- 1 grater
- Cooking spray
- Parchment paper, unbleached kind
- 1 large bowl
- An ice cream scoop

- Spatula
- 2 large baking sheets

Ingredients to use are:

- 2 large eggs
- 4 grated cloves of garlic
- 1 tsp of dried oregano
- 2 tbsp of onion powder
- 2 pounds of ground turkey
- 1 cup of grated zucchini
- Salt and ground black pepper to your preferred taste

Directions for preparation

1. Make sure your oven is preheated to 375°F. Place your parchment paper on the baking sheets and spray some cooking spray on it.

2. Put your ground turkey, zucchinis, eggs, oregano, garlic, onion powder, salt, and pepper in a bowl. Mix these ingredients.

3. Make about 47 meatballs from the mixture in the bowl with your ice cream scoop and place on your oiled baking sheets.

4. Let the meatballs bake in the oven for 15 minutes. Turn the meatballs with your spatula and bake for another 5 minutes.

Note:

Steak Burritos

(Time: 30 minutes)

Nutritional value per serving

One serving contains:

- 31 grams of protein

- 49 grams of carbohydrates - 7 grams of fiber

- 16 grams of fat - 6 grams of saturated fat

- 4 grams of sugar

- 62 milligrams of cholesterol

- 603 milligrams of sodium

- 472 calories

Total servings: 4

Utensils to use are:

- 1 grater

- 1 medium sized kitchen knife

- 1 small saucepan

- 1 large skillet

Ingredients to are:

- 2 tbsp of chopped cilantro

- ½ cup of shredded cheddar cheese

- ½ cup of fresh salsa

- ½ cup of ready guacamole

- 15 oz of low-sodium black beans

- ¼ cup of instant brown rice

- 4 whole wheat tortillas

- 12 oz of thin sliced (crosswise) strip steak

- 1 tbsp of canola oil

- ¼ tsp of ground pepper

Directions for preparation

1. In your saucepan, mix salsa and some water, and boil over medium-low heat.

2. Next add your brown rice and, after 5 minutes of simmering, add your black beans. Let it cook for five more minutes, while your stir the contents of the pan from time to time.

3. Put oil in a skillet and let it get hot over medium-high heat. Put some salt on your steak and place it in the oil. Cook until the steak is brown on every side. This may take up to 5 minutes.

4. Cut your steak and add to each tortilla. On top of that, place cilantro, guacamole, and cheddar cheese. Roll tortillas into burritos.

Note:

Mustard-Maple Pork Tenderloin

(Time: 30 minutes)

Nutritional value per serving

One serving contains:

- 24 grams of protein

- 5 grams of fat - 1 gram of saturated fat

- 9 grams of carbohydrates - 0 grams of fiber

- 74 milligrams of cholesterol

- 472 milligrams of sodium

- 6 grams of sugar

- 186 calories

Total servings: 4

Utensils to use are:

- 1 chopping board

- 1 medium sized kitchen knife

- 1 small bowl

- 1 large oven-proof, non-stick see

- 1 wooden spoon

- 1 whisk

- A thermometer

Ingredients to use are:

- 1 ½ tsp of chopped fresh sage

- 1 pound of trimmed pork tenderloin

- 2 tbsp of maple syrup

- 2 tsp of canola oil

- ¼ cup cider vinegar

- Kosher salt and freshly ground pepper as preferred

Directions for preparation

1. Ensure your oven is preheated to 425°F.

2. In a small bowl, put salt, pepper, and a tbsp of mustard. Mix them and rub it on the pork. Place your skillet over medium-high heat and put the canola oil in it. When the oil is hot, put your pork in it and cook until it is brown. This should take up to 5 minutes. Put the skillet in the oven and roast your pork for about 12 minutes. Use a thermometer placed inside the center of the pork to check if the temperature of the pork is up to 145°F. If it is, then set the pork aside on a chopping board.

3. Place the skillet back on your stove that is set to medium-high heat and add some vinegar. Let vinegar boil and, using a wooden spoon, take out some of the bits and pieces left behind by the pork. This shouldn't take longer than 20 minutes.

4. Next, put in your maple syrup and what is left of your mustard and whisk. Leave them to boil. Turn the heat down to medium and let it simmer for five minutes.

5. Add some sage to the sauce. Cut the pork and top with sauce.

Note:

Skillet Ravioli Lasagna

(Time: 20 minutes)

Nutritional value per serving

2 ½ cups contains:

- 38 grams of protein

- 33 grams of carbohydrates - 3 grams of fiber

- 20 grams of fat - 11 grams of saturated fat

- 127 milligrams of cholesterol

- 5 grams of sugar

- 630 milligrams of sodium

- 483 calories

Total serving: 6

Utensils to use are:

- Broiler

- Oven appropriate skillet

- 1 large pot

- 1 wooden spoon

- 1 colander

Ingredients to use are:

- 24 oz of frozen cheese ravioli

- 8 oz of small and fresh mozzarella balls

- 1 pound of ground lean beef

- ¼ cup of chopped fresh basil

- 1 ½ tsp of dried oregano

- 28 oz of crushed tomatoes, without added salt

- ½ tsp of garlic powder

- Ground pepper and salt to your desired taste

Directions for preparation

1. Make sure to preheat your broiler.

2. Place your pot containing salted water on a stove that is set to medium-high heat. Cook your ravioli in accordance with the cooking instructions on the package. Drain the ravioli and keep it aside for later.

3. Place your oven appropriate skillet over medium-high heat and put your beef in it. Cook it for 5 minutes, all the while breaking down the beef with your wooden spoon. Add some oregano, salt, pepper, and garlic powder to season the beef. Also

add tomatoes and basil, then reduce the heat to medium and let it simmer.

4. Put in ½ of the mozzarella balls and your ravioli into the pan and fold them well together.

5. Sprinkle the rest of the mozzarella balls on the top of the ravioli and place the pan in the broiler with care. Cook for 3 minutes.

Note:

Broccoli Beef

(Time: 30 minutes)

Nutritional value per servings

One serving contains:

- 3.2 grams of total fat

- 19.2 grams of protein

- 755 milligrams of sodium

- 19 grams of total carbohydrates

- 39 milligrams of cholesterol

- 178 calories

Total Servings: 4

Utensils to use are:

- Skillet (large size) — To cook the ingredients

- Spatula — To stir and flip the ingredients

- Bowl — To hold the ingredients

Ingredients to use are:

- 1 pound of round steak, cut into bite size pieces (boneless variety)

- 4 cups of fresh broccoli, chopped

- 2 tablespoons of soy sauce

- 1/4 cup of flour (all-purpose)

- 2 tablespoons of white sugar

- 1/4 teaspoon of fresh ginger root, chopped

- 1 garlic clove, minced

- 1 can of beef broth (10.5 ounce)

Directions for preparation

1. Get a small bowl. Pour in flour and broth. Drizzle with soy sauce and sprinkle with sugar. Stir until the flour and sugar mix evenly.

2. Place a wok or skillet (large size) over the cooker. Turn the heat on high and proceed to cook the beef for about 2 to 4 minutes. Stir regularly until it becomes brown.

3. Pour in the broth mixture and add the broccoli, garlic, and ginger. Turn down the heat and allow to boil.

4. Simmer for about 5 to 10 minutes, or until the sauce reaches your desired thickness.

Note:

Tenderloin Steak Diane

(Time: 30 minutes)

Nutritional value per serving

One serving contains:

- 21 grams of total fat —11 grams of saturated fat

- 111 milligrams of cholesterol

- 2 grams of total carbohydrate — 1 gram of total sugars, and 0 gram of dietary fibre

- 567 milligrams of sodium

- 358 calories

Total servings: 4

Utensils for use are:

- Skillet (large size) — To cook the ingredients

- Spatula — To stir and flip the ingredients

- Bowl — To hold the ingredients

Ingredients to use are:

- 1 teaspoon of chives, minced

- 1 teaspoon of steak seasoning

- 1 cup of fresh mushrooms, sliced

- 1 teaspoon of garlic salt with parsley

- 1/4 cup of whipping cream (heavy variety)

- 1 tablespoon of steak sauce

- 2 tablespoons of butter

- 1/2 cup of beef broth, reduced-sodium

- 4 beef tenderloin steaks (6 ounces each)

Directions for preparation

1. Sprinkle the steak seasoning over the steaks. Proceed to get a skillet (large size) and place over the cooker.

2. Melt butter in the skillet over medium heat. add your steaks into the skillet to cook.

3. Cook for about 4 to 5 minutes until your desired doneness is achieved. Turn over to cook each side.

4. Remove the steak into a bowl with a spatula. Proceed to pour in the mushroom to the skillet to cook over medium-high heat. Stir regularly until it cooks and becomes tender.

5. Stir in the broth to loosen the parts that have turned brown. Add the steak sauce and cream. Sprinkle with garlic salt to taste.

6. Allow to cook while stirring occasionally until the sauce attains your desired thickness.

7. Replace the steaks back into the skillet, and turn over with a spatula to evenly coat and cook while adding the chives.

Note:

Honey Garlic Pork Chops

(Time: 22 minutes)

Nutritional value per serving

One serving contains:

- 12 grams of total fat — 5 grams of saturated fat

- 29 grams of protein

- 15 grams of total carbohydrates

- 104 milligrams of cholesterol

- 68 milligrams of sodium

- 332 calories

Total servings: 4

Ingredients to use are:

- 1/4 cup of honey

- Salt and pepper, to season

- 6 cloves of garlic, minced

- 1 teaspoon of garlic powder

- 2 tablespoons of olive oil

- 2 tablespoons of rice wine vinegar (or apple cider vinegar, or any white variety of vinegar)

- 1 tablespoon of butter (unsalted)

- 1/4 cup of water or chicken broth

- 4 pork chops, bone in or out

Directions for preparation

1. Preheat an oven to 390°F over medium-high heat. Sprinkle garlic powder, pepper and salt over chops before beginning to cook.

2. Place a skillet over the cooker. Pour in oil to heat over medium-high heat before adding the seasoned chops.

3. Flip both sides of the chops to sear evenly for 4 to 5 minutes until it cooks through and turns golden brown.

4. Remove the chops with a spatula and set on a plate.

5. Turn down the heat to medium and add butter to the skillet to melt. Scrape out the browned parts from the pan, and sauté the garlic for 30 seconds until it gives off its fragrance.

6. Pour in water, honey, and vinegar, and turn up the heat to medium-high or high heat. Cook for 3

to 4 minutes until the sauce has reduced and becomes thick. Stir regularly.

7. Replace the pork back into the skillet and apply a generous amount of sauce to it by basting. Broil for about 1 to 2 minutes until the ends begin to char slightly.

8. Finish by garnishing with parsley. Can be served with salads or over pasta, rice, and vegetables.

Note:

Greek Herbed Lamb

(Time: 30 minutes)

Nutritional value per serving

One serving contains:

- 57.7 grams of total fat

- 34.1 grams of protein

- 16.5 grams of total carbohydrates — 6.4 grams of dietary fibre

- 714.5 calories

Total Servings: 4

Utensils to use are:

- 1 juicer

- 1 medium sized kitchen knife

- 1 chopping board

- 1 saucepan

- 1 small jug

- 1 ziplock bag

Ingredients to use are:

For the lamb

- 1 lemon, juiced (2 tbsp)
- Lamb tenderloin fillet (1.5 pound)
- 1 tsp of dried parsley
- 1/4 tsp of pepper
- 2 tsp of dried oregano
- 2-3 cloves of garlic (crushed)
- 1 tbsp of olive oil (extra virgin variety)

Cauliflower mash

- Himalayan salt
- 1 oz unsalted butter chopped
- 1 cup light cream
- 3 cups chicken broth
- 2 pounds of cauliflower chopped

Directions for preparation

To prepare the mash

1. Get a saucepan and place over heat. Pour in some chicken stock and cream and mix evenly.

2. Break off the cauliflower's florets into the saucepan. Allow to boil and turn down the heat. Cover and let simmer for 15 minutes.

3. Proceed with the lamb marinade

To make the lamb marinade

1. Get a small jug and pour in all the ingredients needed asides the lamb. Mix thoroughly.

2. Put the lamb into a ziplock bag and pour in the marinade. Zip the bag shut and work the bag to coat the lamb well.

3. Allow to sit and marinate for 10 minutes.

4. Get a frying pan and place over the cooker. Pour in 1 tbsp of oil to heat over medium-high heat.

5. Pour in the lamb to cook for about 3 to 4 minutes.

6. Drain the cauliflower while the lamb cooks. It should be tender already. Reserve 1/4 cup of the cauliflower's liquid.

7. Pour in the reserved liquid, butter, cauliflower and salt into a food processor. Blitz until a puree is formed. You can also use an immersion blender.

8. Serve the cauliflower puree with the lamb.

Note:

Salisbury Steak with Mushroom Gravy

(Time: 30 minutes)

Nutritional value per serving

One serving contains:

- 13 grams of total fat — 5 grams of saturated fat

- 15 grams of carbohydrates — 4 grams of sugar, and 1 gram of fibre

- 25 grams of protein

- 101 milligrams of cholesterol

- 286 calories

Total servings: 3

Utensils to use are:

- Skillet — To cook the ingredients

- Spatula — To stir and remove ingredients

- Bowl — To hold the ingredients

- Grater — To grate the onion

Ingredients to use are:

Salisbury steak

- 1 egg

- 1/2 onion (white, brown or yellow)

- 1 lb/500g ground beef (i.e. beef mince)

- 3 tsp of dijon mustard OR 2 tsp dry mustard powder

- 1 clove of garlic, minced

- 1/2 cup of panko breadcrumbs (or 1/3 cup ordinary breadcrumbs)

- 2 tbsp of ketchup

- 1 beef bouillon cube, crumbled

- 1/2 tsp of Worcestershire sauce

Gravy

- 2 tsp of Worcestershire sauce

- 2 tsp of dijon mustard

- 2 garlic cloves, minced

- 1 cup of water

- 5 oz/150g mushrooms, sliced

- 2 tbsp of unsalted butter

- 2 cups of beef stock

- 3 tbsp of plain flour

- 1/2 onion, finely chopped

- Salt and pepper

- 1 tbsp of olive oil

Directions for preparation

To make the Salisbury steak

1. Get a bowl and place the breadcrumbs in it. Proceed to grate the onion over breadcrumbs with a box grater. Use your fingers to mix both ingredients, and allow to sit.

2. Add the remaining ingredients for the Salisbury Steak into a bowl and work to mix well.

3. Divide the mixture into 5 oval patties measuring 3/4" / 1 2/3 cm thick.

To prepare the gravy

1. Place a skillet over a cooker. Pour in oil to heat over high heat. Put in the steaks to cook for 1 minute on each side. Cook until the steaks become brown.

2. Use a spatula to take out the steaks and move them onto a plate.

3. Add more oil to the skillet if the oil used in frying the steaks decreases. Proceed to add in the

onion and garlic. Allow to cook for about 2 minutes until they become translucent.

4. Put the mushrooms into the skillet to cook for about 2 to 3 minutes until they become golden brown.

5. Turn down the heat to medium, and melt the butter in the skillet. Stir in the flour and cook for about 30 seconds.

6. Stir in the beef broth gradually until smooth and free of lumps. Add the other ingredients for the gravy.

7. Next, pour in the gravy and the liquid with it. Leave to cook for 5 to 7 minutes until the gravy begins to thicken. Stir regularly around the steaks.

8. If the gravy thickens quickly, add some water. Remove the steak to a plate, and taste to adjust pepper and salt as desired.

9. Top the Salisbury steaks with the gravy. Best served with mashed potatoes. Sprinkle with parsley if you want.

Note:

Chapter 6:

Healthy Chicken Recipes

Thank you for choosing this recipe book,
I hope it is useful for you.

I would like
have your own opinion on the recipes
you are going to prepare.
Your help will help me to improve
and deepen the arguments.

I thank you in advance if you want to help me
and enjoy your work.

Potato and Chicken Sausage Hash Topped with Eggs

(Time: 30 minutes)

Nutritional Value per serving

One serving contains:

- 23 grams of protein

- 25 grams of total fats — 6 grams of saturated fat

- 1045 milligrams of sodium

- 446 calories

- 27 grams of total carbohydrates — 2 grams of dietary fibre and 4 grams of total sugars

- 264 milligrams of cholesterol

Total servings: 4

Utensils to use are:

- 2 large Skillets (Non-stick variety) — for frying

- Spatula — To stir

- Knife and Chopping board — To chop the pepper and onions

- Bowls — To hold chopped up ingredients

- Perforated spoon

- Large spoon (Regular kitchen variety) — To scoop the veggies

- Sieve — To drain the cooked pasta

Ingredients to use are:

- 4 large eggs

- 1 tbsp of butter

- 1 tbsp and 2 tbsp of canola oil (separated)

- Half a cup of chopped sweet onions

- Half a cup of chopped roasted, sweet red pepper

- ¼ tsp and ⅛ tsp of pepper (separated)

- 1 packet of fully cooked, sun-dried, and coarsely chopped tomato chicken sausage links or any other flavour you prefer (12 ounces)

- 1 packet of diced potatoes and onion, refrigerated (20 ounces)

Directions for preparation

1. Heat one large skillet (non-stick) over medium heat and pour in 1 tbsp of canola oil.

2. Add chopped sausages to the oil as it heats. Allow to cook for 4 to 6 minutes until browned lightly. Stir regularly.

3. Remove the cooked sausages with a perforated spoon.

4. Add the remaining 2 tbsp of canola oil to the already heated skillet.

5. Add chopped sweet onions, potatoes and ¼ tsp of pepper. Cover and cook for 10 to 12 minutes until golden brown coloration is achieved. Stir potatoes regularly.

6. Add the sausage and red pepper by stirring in. Cover to cook.

7. Heat a second skillet (nonstick) over medium heat. Pour in the butter to melt.

8. Break the eggs into the pan one at a time. Turn down the heat to low. Cover and cook for 5 to 6 minutes until the yolks begin to thicken, and the egg whites are completely set.

9. You can also turn over the eggs using a spatula, cooking the flipped side to your desired doneness.

10. Turn off the heat cooking the eggs. Sprinkle the remaining ⅛ tsp of pepper over the eggs.

11. Serve eggs over the potato and chicken sausage hash.

Note:

_____

_____

_____

_____

_____

_____

_____

Mediterranean Chicken

(Time: 25 minutes)

Nutritional value per serving

One serving contains:

- 28.6 grams of protein

- 7.2 grams of carbohydrates

- 6.2 grams of fat

- 268 milligrams of sodium

- 68 milligrams of cholesterol

- 222 calories

Total Servings: 6

Utensils to use are:

- 1 chopping board

- 1 medium sized kitchen knife

- 1 large skillet

Ingredients to use are:

- ¼ cup of diced parsley

- 2 tsp of olive oil

- ½ cup of Kalamata olives

- 2 tbsp of white wine, plus ½ cup

- 1 tbsp of diced basil

- 6 chicken breasts, without skin or bones

- 2 tsp of diced fresh thyme

- 3 chopped cloves of garlic

- 3 cups of diced tomatoes

- Salt and pepper to taste

- ½ cup of chopped onions

Directions for preparation

1. Put 2 tbsp of wine in your skillet and add oil to it. Then place the skillet on your stove that has already been set to medium-high heat. Put your chicken in the pan and for 6 minutes, saute it. By the end of the 6 minutes, your chicken should have turned golden brown. Remove it and keep it for later.

2. Now, put your garlic, onions, and tomatoes in the skillet and let them cook for 3 minutes. Make sure to stir as they cook. Reduce the heat to medium-low and add what is left of your white wine, thyme, and basil. Let it cook for 5 minutes.

3. After that, put your chicken back in the skillet and let it cool through. Cover your skillet while the chicken simmers. Add some salt, pepper, olives, and parsley to the chicken and cook for another minute.

Note:

Chicken Stew

(Time: 20 minutes)

Nutritional value per serving

One serving contains:

- 4 grams of fat - 1 gram of saturated fat

- 22 grams of carbohydrates - 5 grams of fiber

- 25 grams of protein

- 5 grams of sugar

- 55 milligrams of cholesterol

- 744 milligrams of sodium

- 214 calories

Total Servings: 4

Utensils to use are:

- 1 large skillet, non-stick kind

- 1 small bowl

- 1 medium sized kitchen knife

- 1 chopping board

- 1 whisk

Ingredients to use are:

- ⅓ cup of all purpose flour

- 2 chicken breasts without skin or bones, cut into tiny pieces

- ½ cup of milk

- 1 cup of a chopped onion

- 1 ½ cups of chicken broth

- 3 chopped stalks of celery

- A pinch of poultry seasoning

- 8 quartered button mushrooms

- 1 ½ tsp of dried thyme

- 2 cups of chopped carrots

- 4 diced cloves of garlic

- 2 tsp of olive oil

- 2 cups of broccoli florets

- ½ tsp of salt and black pepper, or to your desired taste

Directions for preparation

1.Place the skillet over your stove which has already been set to medium heat. Put the olive oil in the pan and add your chicken. Cook the chicken for 3 minutes before adding your already chopped onions, broccoli, mushrooms, and carrots. Also, add garlic, thyme, poultry seasoning, pepper, and salt to the chicken and stir it well for another 3 minutes. Pour the chicken broth into the pan and stir.

2. Get your bowl and put milk and flour in it. Whisk thoroughly and add to the pan. Do not pour it on the chicken or vegetables. Push those to a corner of the pan. Only pour the milk mixture into the broth.

3. Once that is done, you can now mix everything together. Reduce the heat to low, cover the pan, and let the contents of the skillet simmer for 12 minutes.

Note:

Chicken Tikka Burritos

(Time: 30 minutes)

Nutritional value per serving

One serving contains:

- 28.7 grams of protein
- 52.2 grams of carbohydrates - 3 grams of fiber
- 7.9 grams of fat - 2.7 grams of saturated fat
- 8 grams of sugar
- 400 calories

Total Servings: 4

Utensils to use are:

- 1 chopping board
- 1 medium sized kitchen knife
- Food processor
- 1 bowl
- Metal skewers

Ingredients to use are:

- 4 warmed rotis

- 4 tbsp of natural yogurt, low-fat

- 1 cup of spicy pilau rice

- 1 juiced lemon

- 1 handful of sliced cherry tomatoes

- 2 chopped cloves of garlic

- Finely chopped ½ onions

- 1 diced ginger

- ½ tsp of garam masala

- 1 chopped green chili, seeds removed

- ¾ tsp of chilli powder

- ½ bunch of chopped coriander, leaves removed

- 1 ½ tsp of smoked paprika

- 2 large chicken breasts, cut in pieces and skin and bones removed

Directions for preparation

1. In a food processor, put lemon juice, ginger, yogurt, coriander stalks, garlic, and green chili. Turn on the food processor and blend until the mixture is smooth. Turn this mixture into your bowl and add your spices. Season the mixture and put the chicken inside it. Mix it thoroughly and set it aside to marinate for a total of 30 minutes. Put

the contents of the bowl into 4 metal skewers and put them on your grill.

2. Before that, line your baking sheet with tin foil and put your skewers on it. Make sure there is some gap between each skewer. Grill for 4 minutes until it is cooked through.

3. Now, mix your onions and cherry tomatoes in a bowl and squeeze some lemon into it. Also, add some seasoning to it. Get another bowl and put in your coriander stalks, yogurt, and lemon juice. Again, add some seasoning.

4. Cook your rice and put it in the four rotis. Put the contents of the two bowls in it and mix.

Note:

_____

_____

_____

_____

_____

_____

Roast Chicken and Sweet Potatoes

(Time: 30 minutes)

Nutritional value per serving

One serving contains:

- 27 grams of protein
- 34 grams of carbohydrates - 5 grams of fiber
- 17 grams of fat - 4 grams of saturated fat
- 12 grams of sugar
- 86 milligrams of cholesterol
- 554 milligrams of sodium
- 408 calories

Total servings: 4

Utensils to use are:

- 1 chopping board
- 1 medium sized kitchen knife
- 2 small bowl

- Thin foil

Ingredients to use are:

- 1 finely diced large red onion

- 2 tbsp of Dijon mustard

- 2 peeled and chopped medium sweet potatoes

- 2 tsp of chopped dried thyme

- 1 ½ pounds of chicken thighs with bones but skinless

- 2 tbsp of organic olive oil

- ½ tsp of salt and freshly ground pepper respectively, or to your preferred taste

Directions for preparation

1. Make sure our oven is heated to 450°F. Then, put your baking sheet that has been rimmed with foil in the middle rack of the oven to be preheated.

2. Get your bowl and put thyme, a tbsp of oil, mustard, and a pinch of salt and pepper in it. Mix this well before using it to coat the chicken.

3. Put 1 tbsp of olive oil and a pinch of salt and pepper in another bowl. Add your chopped potatoes and onions, and toss well.

4. With care, take your baking sheet from the oven and transfer the contents of the bowl onto it. Put your chicken on the baking sheet and put it back in the oven to roast. It should take about 25 minutes before the potatoes and onions start to brown and get tender.

Note:

Greek Cauliflower Rice Bowls with Grilled Chicken

(Time: 30 minutes)

Nutritional value per serving

One serving contains:

- 29 grams of protein

- 9 grams of carbohydrates - 3 grams of fiber

- 28 grams of fat - 4 grams of saturated fat

- 5 grams of sugar

- 630 milligrams of sodium

- 87 milligrams of cholesterol

- 411 calories

Total servings: 4

Utensils to use are:

- A food processor

- 1 chopping board

- 1 medium sized kitchen knife

- 1 large skillet

- 1 thermometer, instant-read

- 1 whisk

- 1 small bowl and 4 large ones

Ingredients to use are:

- 2 tbsp of feta cheese, crumbled

- 6 ⅓ tbsp of Extra Virgin olive oil

- 2 tbsp of Kalamata olives, diced

- 4 cups of processed cauliflower florets

- 1 cup of diced cucumber

- ⅓ cups of diced red onions

- 1 cup of cherry tomatoes, cut in halves

- ¾ tsp of salt

- 1 tsp of dried oregano

- ½ cup of diced fresh dill

- 1 pound of chicken breasts, without bones or skin

- 3 tbsp of lemon juice

- ½ tsp of ground pepper

Directions for preparation

5. Ensure your grill is pre-set to medium heat

6. Place your skillet on a stove set to medium-high heat and put some oil in it. Add onions, ¼ tsp of salt, and cauliflower granules. It should take about 5 minutes for the cauliflower to become soft. After that, take the skillet off the heat and add ¼ cup of dill. Stir it well.

7. Coat your chicken in your a tsp of oil and sprinkle about ¼ tsp of salt and pepper on it. Grill the chicken for about 15 minutes. Make sure to turn it once 7 minutes into the grilling. A thermometer inserted into the chicken breast should read 165°F.

8. Put lemon juice, 4 tbsp of oil, oregano, and what remains of your salt and pepper into a bowl. Beat with a whisk until they are well mixed.

9. Divide the cauliflower granules into 4 separate bowls. Place your grilled chicken, feta cheese, olives, tomatoes, and diced cucumber on the rice. Sprinkle what is left of your dill and some vinaigrette on the rice.

Note:

Chapter 7:

Healthy Dessert

Recipes

Thank you for choosing this recipe book,
I hope it is useful for you.

,

I would like
have your own opinion on the recipes
you are going to prepare.
Your help will help me to improve
and deepen the arguments.

I thank you in advance if you want to help me
and enjoy your work.

Strawberry Lemon Shortcakes

(Time: 30 minutes)

Nutritional value per servings

One serving contains:

- 21 grams of total fat — 13 grams of saturated fat

- 6 grams of protein

- 47 grams of total carbohydrates — 2 grams of fibre, and 21 grams of total sugars

- 106 milligrams of cholesterol

- 394 calories

Total servings: 4

Utensils to use are:

- Oven — For baking

- Bowl (small size) — To mix ingredients

- Bowl (large size) — To mix ingredients for the shortcake

- Whisk — To mix ingredients

- Baking sheet — To hold the dough

- Parchment paper — To line the baking sheet

Ingredients to use are:

General ingredients:

- 1 to 1 ½ cups sliced fresh strawberries
- 2 tablespoons of sugar
- ¼ tsp of grated lemon zest
- 1 tbsp of softened butter

Ingredients for the shortcake:

- 1 egg yolk (large variety)
- ⅛ tsp of salt
- ¾ tsp lemon zest, grated
- 3 tablespoons of sugar
- ⅓ cups of 2% milk
- 1 cup of flour (all-purpose variety)
- 1 tsp of baking powder
- 3 tablespoons of cold butter, cut into cubes

Ingredients for whipped cream

- 1 tsp of sugar
- ⅓ cup of whipping cream (heavy variety)

1. Preheat the oven to a temperature of 450°F. Get a bowl (small sized) and pour in ¼ tsp of grated lemon zest and 1 tbsp of softened butter.

2. Get another bowl (small size) and add about ½ to 1 cup of fresh strawberry slices. Sprinkle with 2 tbsp of sugar, and toss to mix. Allow to sit while you proceed to prepare the shortcakes.

3. Get a bowl (large size) and pour in 1 cup of all-purpose flour, 1 tsp of baking powder, 3 tbsp of sugar, and ¾ tsp of grated lemon zest. Sprinkle with ⅛ tsp of salt to taste.

4. Beat the mixture with a whisk until well blended. Proceed to add 3 tbsp of cold butter sliced into cubes. Whisk until the mixture attains a texture comparable to coarse crumbs.

5. Break 1 large egg and remove the yolk into another large bowl. Add ⅓ cups of milk, and beat the milk and yolk mix until completely blended.

6. Stir in the yolk and milk mix into the flour mix until well moistened.

7. Lightly flour a clean, flat surface for kneading. Proceed to knead the dough about 4 to 5 times. Divide the dough into portions (about 4).

8. Place each portion of dough into a ¾ inches thick circle stationed 2 inches apart on a baking sheet lined with parchment paper.

9. Place the dough into the oven and bake for about 8 to 10 minutes until the dough begins to turn golden brown.

10. Transfer the baked shortcakes from the pan to a wire rack to cool.

11.Get another bowl (small size). In it, pour ⅓ cup of whipping cream (heavy variety). Beat with a whisk until the cream gradually begins to become thick.

12. Sprinkle with 1 tsp of sugar, and continue to beat with a whisk until soft peaks form in the mix.

13. Halve the shortcakes when serving, and top the bottom parts with strawberry slices and whipped cream. Spread the butter and lemon zest mix on the top part, and place over the strawberry slices.

Note:

Chocolate Chip Oatmeal Cookies

(Time: 20 minutes)

Nutritional value per servings

One serving (1 cookie) contains:

- 5 grams of total fat — 2 grams of saturated fat

- 1 gram of protein

- 11 grams of total carbohydrates — 1 gram of fibre and 7 grams of sugar

- 84 milligrams of sodium

- 87 calories

Total servings: 7 dozen (84 cookies)

Utensils to use are:

- Bowl (large size) — To mix the ingredients

- Whisk — To mix ingredients

- Baking sheets (ungreased) — To hold cookies

- Oven — To bake cookies

Ingredients to use:

- ¾ cup of sugar

- 1 packet of instant vanilla pudding mix (3.4 ounces)

- 1 tsp of vanilla extract

- 2 eggs (large variety)

- 1 cup of chopped nuts

- 1 tsp of salt

- 3 cups of oats (quick-cooking variety)

- ¾ cup of packed brown sugar

- 1 cup of softened butter

- 2 cups of chocolate chips (12 ounces) (semisweet variety)

- 1 tsp of baking soda

Direction for preparation

1. Get a large bowl and add 1 cup of softened butter and ¾ cup of sugar. Beat to form a light and fluffy mix.

2. Break 2 large eggs into the mix, and drizzle with 1 tsp of vanilla extract. Beat with a whisk until well combined.

3. Get another bowl and pour in 1 packet of instant vanilla pudding mix, 3 cups of quick-cooking oats,

1 tsp of baking soda, flour, and 1 tsp of salt. Work until well combined.

4. Proceed to stir the dry mix into the creamed mixture, and mix thoroughly. Add 1 cup of chopped nuts and 2 cups of chocolate chips, and mix well.

5. Get some ungreased baking sheets and divide the dough into balls 2 inches apart.

6. Set the oven at 375°F and bake for 10 to 12 minutes until the cookies begin to brown slightly.

7. Remove the cookies onto wire racks to cool.

Note:

Apple Rings

(Time: 25 minutes)

Nutritional value per serving

One serving contains:

- 1 gram of total fat — 0 gram of saturated fat

- 77 milligrams of Sodium

- 2 grams of protein

- 184 milligrams of potassium

- 35 grams of total carbohydrates — 2 grams of dietary fiber, and 22 grams of total sugars

- 19 milligrams Cholesterol

- 162 Calories

Total servings 10

Utensils to use are:

- Bowl (small size) — To mix the ingredients

- Whisk — For mixing ingredients

- Skillet (large size) — To fry apple slices

- Knife or Cookie cutter — To cut ingredients round apple slices

Ingredients to use are:

- ¼ tsp of baking powder

- 1 egg (large size)

- 1 cup of flour (all-purpose variety)

- ½ cup of sugar

- ¼ tsp of salt

- canola oil for frying

- 1 cup of plain yogurt

- 6 cooking apples, sliced into ¼ inches thick slices

- 1 to 2 teaspoons cinnamon

Directions for preparation

1.Get a small mixing bowl and pour in ¼ tsp of baking powder and 1 cup of flour. Sprinkle with salt. Mix thoroughly with a whisk and let sit.

2. Get another bowl and break in 1 large egg. Pour in 1 cup of plain yogurt and beat with a whisk to combine thoroughly.

3. Pour in the egg and yogurt mix into the flour mixture and beat with a whisk. Let sit.

4. Cut 6 cooking apples into slices, and cut rings out of the centre of each slice using a knife or cookie cutter

5. Get a skillet (large size) and place over medium-low heat reaching up to 375°F. Pour in the canola oil to heat up.

6. Dip the cutout apple rings into the flour mixture, and place into the oil to fry. Cook in batches for about 1 to 2 minutes per slice until golden brown. Turn over to cook each side.

7. Get a small bowl or plate and pour in 1 to 2 teaspoons cinnamon. Sprinkle with ½ cup of sugar. Work to mix well.

8. Drizzle the sugar and cinnamon mixture over the apple rings. Best served hot.

Note:

Rice Crispy Treat Bark

(Time: 30 minutes)

Nutritional value per serving

One serving contains:

- 0.7 grams of total fat

- 15.3grams of total carbohydrates — 0.0 gram of dietary fibre

- 83.2 milligrams of sodium

- 0.5 grams of protein

- milligram of cholesterol

- 47.1 Calories

Total Servings: 3

Utensils for use are:

- Baking dish (8 x 8) — For baking

- Bowl (medium sized) — To mix ingredients

- Bowl (microwave safe variety) — To heat up bark

- Microwave — To heat ingredients

- Spoon — To stir ingredients

- Parchment paper — To line baking dish

- Plastic wrap — To seal baking dish

- Knife — To cut ingredients

- Spatula — To spread ingredients

Ingredients to use:

- White almond bark (10 ounces)

- ¾ cup of Rice Krispies cereal

- ½ cup of mini marshmallows, torched (A brûlée torch is needed to do this)

- ½ cup of coarsely chopped, frozen, dried strawberries

- 1 tsp of Nielsen-Massey vanilla bean paste

Directions for preparation

1. Get a baking dish measuring 8 x 8 inches. Proceed to line the dish with parchment paper.

2. Get a mixing bowl (medium sized) and pour in ½ cup of coarsely chopped, frozen, dried strawberries, ¾ cup of Rice Krispies cereal and ½ cup of torched mini marshmallows. Mix well.

3. Place the white almond bark into a bowl and microwave. Heat for about 30 seconds until well melted. Stir regularly within intervals.

4. Stir in 1 tsp of Nielsen-Massey vanilla bean paste into the melted white almond bark. Mix well to blend the mixture.

5. Introduce the dry ingredients slowly into the melted almond and vanilla bean paste mixture. Stir well to properly coat the dry mixture.

6. Use a spoon to transfer the mixture onto the baking dish lined with parchment paper.

7. Get a spatula and proceed to distribute the bark mixture evenly in the dish.

8. Use plastic wrap to seal the baking dish. Proceed to put the baking dish into the refrigerator to set.

9. Cut the bark with a kitchen knife and serve.

Note:

S'mores Bars

(Time: 30 minutes)

Nutritional value per serving

One serving contains:

- 17 grams of total fat

- 44 grams of total carbohydrates — 32 grams of total sugars and 1 gram of dietary fibre

- 170 milligrams of sodium

- 2 grams of protein

- 30 milligrams of cholesterol

- 330 calories

Total Servings: 1 baking dish

Utensils to use are:

- Baking dish (9 × 13 inches) — For baking ingredients

- Bowl (microwave safe variety)

- Microwave — To heat ingredients

Ingredients to use are:

- 1 cup of chocolate chips

- 8 cups of golden grahams

- ½ cup of corn syrup

- 4 cups of mini marshmallows

- 4 tbsp of butter (divided)

- Extra marshmallows and chocolate for decoration

Directions for preparation

1. Get a baking dish measuring 9 x 13 inches. Coat the dish with nonstick spray and let sit.

2. Get a microwave safe bowl of medium size and pour in ½ cup of corn syrup, 3 tbsp of butter and 1 cup of chocolate chips.

3. Proceed to insert the bowl into a microwave and heat for roughly 2 minutes until tender.

4. Use a spatula to stir the chocolate mixture until every chunk dissolves and a creamy mixture is

achieved. Remove the chocolate mixture from the microwave and let sit.

5. Place a large pot over medium heat and go on to add the remaining 1 tbsp of butter and 4 cups of mini marshmallows. Allow to cook.

6. Stir regularly as the marshmallows begin to melt. Cook until they melt completely and become gooey.

7. Next, pour in the 8 cups of golden grahams and add the extra chocolate to the large pot in which the marshmallow mixture cooks. Stir well to completely mix the ingredients.

8. Turn off the heat and add in some extra chocolate chips and marshmallows according to your preference.

9. Pour the hot mixture into the set 9 x 13 inch baking dish already coated with nonstick spray. Add more chocolate chips and marshmallows as toppings as you desire.

10. Let sit to set before serving. Refrigerate any leftovers.

Note:

Meyer Lemon Cheesecake Shots

(Time: 20 minutes)

Nutritional value per serving

One serving contains:

- 49 grams of total fat — 17 grams of saturated fat, 10 grams of unsaturated fat, and 2 grams of polyunsaturated fat

- 46 grams of total carbohydrates — 1 gram of dietary fibre

- 609 milligrams of sodium

- 10 grams of protein

- 337 milligrams of cholesterol

- 663 calories

Total servings: 6

Utensils for use are:

- Bowl (medium sized) — To mix the ingredients

- Shot glasses (mini variety) — To hold the shots

- Stand mixer — To beat ingredients

- Piping bag — To fill shot glasses

Ingredients to use are:

For the Base

- 2 tablespoons of melted butter

- 1 cup of graham crumbs

For the Lemon filling

- 2 cups of cool whip

- 1 tsp of Meyer lemon juice

- ½ brick of softened cream cheese

For the blueberry filling

- 1 cup of cool whip

- ¼ cup of crushed fresh blueberries

- ¼ brick of softened cream cheese

For the topping

- 1 cup of cool whip

For the garnish

- Meyer Lemon Zest

- Blueberries

Directions for preparation

To prepare the base

1. Get a bowl (medium sized) and pour in 2 tablespoons of melted butter and 1 cup of graham crumbs. Work to thoroughly mix the ingredients.

2. Proceed to press the crumbs and butter mixture into shot glasses (mini variety) to the bottom.

To prepare the lemon filling

1. Get a stand mixer and pour in 2 cups of cool whip, 1 tsp of Meyer lemon juice, and ½ brick of softened cream cheese. Whisk the mixture until it becomes fluffy.

2. To fill the shot glasses easier and faster, consider moving the mixture into a piping bag.

3. Proceed to fill the shot glasses in any order you like. There is no definite arrangement for making the Meyer lemon cheesecake shots.

To prepare the blueberry filling

1. Get a stand mixer and pour in 1 cup of cool whip, ¼ cup of crushed fresh blueberries, and ¼ brick of softened cream cheese. Whisk the mixture until it becomes fluffy.

2. To fill the shot glasses easier and faster, consider moving the mixture into a piping bag.

3. Proceed to fill the shot glasses in any order you like. There is no definite arrangement for making the Meyer lemon cheesecake shots.

To prepare the topping

1. Place 1 cup of cool whip into a piping bag with a large opening. Pipe the contents over the filling in the shot glasses.

To prepare the garnish:

1. Top the content of the shot glasses with lemon zest or blueberries.

2. Store the drinks in the refrigerator until they are ready to be served.

3. Best serve chilled.

Recipe tips

• Feel free to combine all 5 layers according to your preference.

Note:

Chocolate Cake

(Time: 30 minutes)

Nutritional value per serving:

One serving contains:

- 24 grams of total fat — 4 grams of saturated fat

- 52 grams of total carbohydrates — 25 grams of total sugars, and 7 grams of dietary fibre

- 149 milligrams of sodium

- 7 grams of protein

- 61 milligrams of cholesterol

- 428 calories

Total servings: 8 to 10

Utensils to use are:

- Bowl (medium sized) — To mix the ingredients

- Cake pan — To hold the cake

- Parchment paper: — To line the baking pan

- Whisk — To beat eggs

- Food processor — To blitz ingredients

- Masher — To mash potatoes

- Spoon — To scoop out potatoes

- Knife — To cut ingredients

Ingredients to use:

For the cake

- ½ cup of maple syrup

- ¼ tsp of baking soda

- 1 tsp of vanilla

- 1 cup of sweet potato, mashed

- 3 eggs, lightly whisked

- ½ cup of cocoa powder

- ½ cup of olive oil

- 1 cup of flour (self-raising variety)

- ¼ tsp of salt

For the chocolate mousse ganache

- ½ cup maple syrup

- 2 avocados

- ½ cup of cocoa powder

Directions for preparation

To prepare the cake

1. Get a round cake pan measuring 9 inches. Line the bottom of the pan with parchment paper and spray lightly with oil to coat.

2. Preheat your oven to 180°C or 355°F.

3. Get a fork and begin piercing the sweet potatoes. Place the pierced potatoes into a microwave safe dish and place into the microwave.

4. Turn on the heat on the microwave to high and cook for 6 to 8 minutes until the flesh becomes tender.

5. Retrieve the potatoes from the microwave and cut open along the length with a knife. Use a spoon to scoop out the edible flesh.

6. Put the flesh into a bowl (medium sized) and grab a masher. Mash well to remove lumps. You can also use a food processor to blitz the potatoes for an even smoother mash. Keep aside to cool.

7. Get another bowl and pour in flour, baking soda, and cocoa powder. Sprinkle with salt to taste. Mix to combine ingredients.

8. Break the eggs into a bowl and beat lightly with a whisk. Pour in the oil, maple syrup, and vanilla. Mix thoroughly.

9. Pour the egg mix into the mashed sweet potatoes. Get a wooden spoon and mix until well combined.

10. Pour in the flour mix, and mix to combine properly.

11. Scoop out the batter into the baking pan lined with parchment paper. Proceed to put the pan into the oven and let it bake for about 18 minutes until the top becomes properly cooked, and the center remains a little gooey.

12. Remove the cake from the oven, and allow to sit and cool for about 10 minutes. Go on to place the cake onto a wire rack to air properly.

To prepare the frosting

1. Skin the avocado and blitz in a food processor with maple syrup and cocoa to form a smooth and silky mix.

2. Once the cake cools completely, proceed to spread the frosting generously across the sides and top of the cake.

Recipe tips

- Sweet potatoes of medium size are better suited for this recipe because they produce about a cup when mashed.

- Before taking off the peel and scooping out the flesh from the sweet potatoes, ensure the potatoes are already soft.

- Cook the potatoes for longer if the potatoes aren't already soft after 8 minutes, since cooking time differs across the size of the potatoes.

- The cake can easily be frozen. To do so, wrap the cake well in plastic wrap until it is ready to be defrosted and served.

Note:

Glazed Apple Cinnamon Rolls

(Time: 30 minutes)

Nutritional value per serving

One serving contains:

- 4 grams of total fat — 1 gram of saturated fat

- 16.8 grams of total carbohydrates

- 250 milligrams of sodium

- 1.6 grams of protein

- 0 milligram of cholesterol

- 100 calories

Total servings: 12

Utensils for use are:

- Wire rack — To cool off the rolls

- Muffin pan — To bake the rolls

- Blender — To mix the ingredients

- Saucepan — To cook the ingredients

- Bowl — To mix the ingredients

- Towel — To cover up the dough

- Whisk — To blend the ingredients

Ingredients to use are:

- 1 tsp of vanilla extract

- ½ cup of packed, light brown sugar

- 3 tablespoons of sugar (granulated variety)

- ¾ cup of finely chopped baking apples (about 1 medium apple)

- 3 cups of flour (all-purpose variety)

- 3 tablespoons of unsalted, melted butter

- ¾ cup of apple cider

- 1 and ¼ tsp of ground cinnamon

- 2 eggs, beaten lightly (large variety)

- 2 and ¼ teaspoons of dry active yeast

For the glaze

- 1 tbsp of milk

- ¼ cup of softened cream cheese

- 1 cup of sugar (confectioner's variety)

- 1 tsp of vanilla extract

Directions for preparation

To prepare the rolls

1. Get a saucepan (small sized) and place over medium heat reaching temperatures of 110°F.

2. Proceed to heat the sugar and cider. Mix well and sprinkle with yeast. Stir well to dissolve the yeast. Allow to set for about 5 minutes.

3. Get a bowl (large size) and pour in vanilla extract, yeast mixture, 2 tbsp of butter, and ¼ tsp of cinnamon. Break the egg into the mix and blend properly.

4. Pour in 1 cup of flour and mix with an electric blender on low speed until the mixture blends properly.

5. Blend in the remaining flour by pouring it in slowly until a soft consistency is achieved in the dough.

6. Scoop out the dough onto a surface sprayed lightly with flour. Knead with your hands gently about 5 times.

7. Spread a damp cloth or towel over the dough and let sit for about 5 minutes.

8. Roll out the dough into a rectangle measuring 18 by 6 inches. Spread the dough with the remaining 1 tbsp of butter.

9. Get another bowl, and in it mix 1 tsp of cinnamon and brown sugar. Drizzle the mixture over the dough evenly. Proceed to top off the brown sugar with chopped apples.

10. Begin at the short side to roll up the dough. Pinch shut the seam to seal off the open end. Proceed to divide the rolls into slices of ½ and 1 inches.

11. Put these slices into a muffin pan that is well greased. Cover and leave to set and rise until it doubles in size.

12. Preheat the oven to 375°F and bake the rolls for 13 to 15 minutes until the rolls begin to brown.

13. Remove the rolls from the pan and set on a wire rack to cool.

To prepare the glaze

1. Get a bowl (small sized) and pour in the milk and cream cheese. Drizzle with some vanilla and whisk to blend the mixture.

2. Sprinkle with granulated sugar and whisk gradually and work with whisk to achieve a smooth consistency.

3. Proceed to drizzle the glaze over the rolls.

Note:

Conclusion

The recipes in this book have been tested to determine that they can actually be prepared in the number of minutes written for each of them. They are also healthy. In this book, you will find a recipe for almost any kind of diet. Every chapter was written to assist people who want to eat healthy, but do not want to spend too long making a meal. Hopefully, you have also learned that nothing beats a home cooked meal! Now, have a go at any of the recipes, and let us know if this book has been of help to you.

I am grateful if you would release reviews that will allow me to improve my work.

Other books by Gina Bates

Air Fryer:

Air Fryer recipes for every taste. Food that is easy to make, healthy, and ideal for weight watchers. Low-budget recipes that anyone can cook for family and friends.

It's so easy to cook perfect meals with your fryer, but it's difficult to find the perfect recipes to consistently push through. Do not get bored with your air fryer! This cookbook contains a diverse collection of dishes to suit every taste and preference.

This book includes:

• Great Recipes for Making Tasty Vegetables

• Delicious Seafood

• Juicy Red Meat

• Poultry

• Tips and tricks for the hot air fryer

• Basics and new techniques

You can buy the book on Amazon at this link:

https://www.amazon.com/dp/B085PTB288

Made in the USA
Coppell, TX
22 April 2020